Monologie:
A Woman's Life in Letters

Monologie:
A Woman's Life in Letters

By

Suzanne Rubinstein

AuthorHouse™
1663 Liberty Drive
Bloomington, IN 47403
www.authorhouse.com
Phone: 1 (800) 839-8640

Published by AuthorHouse 01/08/2015

ISBN: 978-1-5882-0384-7 (sc)

Dedication

For Harvey Simms, without whose friendship, insight, probity, wit, and gentle nature, a fine insanity would have gone unsung.

Prologue

TUESDAY, MAY 4TH

I've voluntarily entered 3-K at Mercy Hospital. Sam looks as dehydrated and burnt out as I do— it's hard to tell who is the patient. But it's me who walks down the hall with the nurse and doesn't look back. "I need to be," I say to the nurse. "Cherish her," she murmurs to the aide.

WEDNESDAY, MAY 5TH

I'm dying. My feet prickle as if a thousand shards of glass were strewn across my path. And so it begins, this gradual descent, the process by which I'll become whole again, or so they tell me.

In "loose parts play" today, I discovered what a huge avoidance I have of performance. Sam's music so fat there's no room for mine. I'm used to taking the credit for his talent, but unused to making a sound! Still I like to bump the drum and let the stick resonate in my hand. It's a beginning, I suppose.

Evening. There's really no place to hide. You can run, but you can't hide, isn't that what they say.

THURSDAY, MAY 6TH

What are the uses of disguise aside from the obvious one of spurring the imagination. To bring magic to one's own life as well as to the life of others. The fog lies deep and low outside my window and two mourning doves entwine themselves for my pleasure. This must be madness.

FRIDAY, MAY 7TH

>A poem for the 3-K newsletter:
>so little of life is left to us for deciding,
>so little of what really matters,

(of what really matters)
jouissant

FRIDAY, MAY 7

"The status quo starts with hierarchical thinking. That's the core of everything that's wrong. It comes from the idea that man is above nature. Then its man above woman -- one half of the race serving another; ad infinitum..."

an ecofeminist
Liz Smith's column, Newsday, May 7, 1993

Pieces of my psyche so deeply buried for so long come floating to the top suddenly. I didn't know how much I knew of the world. Today's a free flowing day. Where would I rather be? They took my radio and headset from me. No music today. I suppose "interaction with others" is the prescribed course.

Outside my window is what looks like a ficus or fig tree. Flat, fleshy, shiny leaves. It's a cloudless day. I'd take a walk if I were allowed. I'm entombed in this place and by my own hand. It only requires a self to be free. Yesterday, the stink of death followed me everywhere. But today is better.

SATURDAY, MAY 8

At last! I went outdoors today for the first time in a week. It was a grand excursion.

Evening. Sam will be working at a club this evening with some of his friends. It's good to write with a pen tonight. Pencils have too much drag to them. Today Cara came for the first time - how beautiful she's become. How good it was to recognize her face among all the others here. I hadn't realized how much I'd longed for her until I saw her in this place.

Still and only Saturday, May 8. It is a fact that I fear disfigurement. What must a woman do to herself in the name of beauty? And what if it becomes more than a matter of cosmetics? What if I should need something more? Some better disguise? No, not at this point, I think.

SUNDAY, MAY 9

I miss not having my watch. I'm profoundly disappointed in my marriage. Is it because he's out working and I'm sitting here waiting for the world to answer my call? On Sundays here it is drearily dismal. Everyone wants to be somewhere except for me. I want to be nowhere.

The one unforgivable sin, it seems to me, is the sin of omission. Yet, here I sit writing my most innermost thoughts at the kitchen table on a psychiatric ward. I feel like Jane Austen must have when she wrote her books in plain sight in the parlor. So that's it. To hide I have to become more visible.

Evening. Having a roommate changes things for me. And when I told Jerry K. and Bob M. that I wasn't able to write, they weren't in the least upset. "So don't," they said. As if it didn't matter. As if it weren't the cure.

The measured walk of drug-induced stupor has begun for most of us.

MONDAY, MAY 10

A long uneventful day on the ward with the exception of my doctor's lifting the medication. That was a triumph for me.

TUESDAY, MAY 11

A natural sleep! Dr. Ciaclos clarifies my medication. I'm back to taking Triavil in the evening. Will I take to walking the halls in fits of boredom? I've called my office and left a message for the boss. I'd like to try to get my job back. Bob M. left. I'll miss him very much.

WEDNESDAY, MAY 12

Yesterday Sam and I both contacted my office independently of each other. For me, it was inconceivable that he would call without first advising me. For him, it was simply second nature. This brought up old issues that lie festering between us. I'm uncomfortable in his presence. I'm trying to arrange some other way out of here. The days pass so slowly here. I must tell my doctor that I've earned privileges. I'm now at what they call "level five."

Evening. Sam and I tried going out for a walk on the grounds this evening. Not too successful. I'm disinterested and he's self involved.

THURSDAY, MAY 13

A red letter day for me. A peaceful night and then Ciaclos suggested we (Sam and I) see Savarino together. Well, I showed my temper and so here I remain while the world moves on to other things. I was saddened to read in *The New Yorker* of Irving Howe's death. He was a mentor even though I never knew him.

FRIDAY, MAY 14

A restful night and someone taking my pulse this morning even before I was awake! It was 98, they said. I woke at ten to seven, showered, and then breakfast was later than it's ever been. Somehow I don't question these things or the competence of the staff. They do their best, I suppose. In retrospect, they don't kill you or cure you. At times, I can hardly tell them from the patients.

I saw Dr. Bernard for the first time today. He said I would have to stay for nine more days! Nine more days! It seems an eternity and I'm losing two more friends tomorrow.

SATURDAY, MAY 15

Last night I dreamt I lost my job because of this damn hospitalization. Interesting that the dream came right after Sam's performance here last evening. I lost my job in the dream because I was unable to perform.

One hour off the unit with Sam. I doubt that this relationship is going anywhere. He's so confused. I'm not used to his being this way.

SUNDAY, MAY 16

Early morning. I grow very weary of medication. It seems to me I'm being manipulated by substances foreign to my body, that my mood is being artificially altered, that I'm a toy for supercilious doctors. Poor, poor Sam -- his search for his father is relentless. He harbors hostile feelings towards the nurses here.

Afternoon. Today is the first day I feel completely myself. They've lightened the medication and I'm back to myself. Now a long week of recuperation.

MONDAY, MAY 17

I woke this morning at the same time: 7:10 a.m. with nothing particular on my mind. The doctor referred to himself and me as "obsessive-compulsive" yesterday. I doubt that's accurate in my case. I'm too adaptive to obsess over much in this world.

Today's the day I must call work. Well, I've left a message. Had a very good one-on-one today with Doris -- spoke to Sam several times. I can't put him off any longer. He's coming over tomorrow afternoon. I feel tonight as if I'm languishing here in the hospital. But where is home?

TUESDAY, MAY 18

I *am* languishing in this place. Many new admissions and I feign disinterest because in reality it's time for me to move on. They'll continue to check into this place in search of sanity. My future remains uncertain. I'm remarkably calm in the face of so much necessity. Sam has insisted on visiting me today. It's a question whether he'll show up with Lennie or not. I'm not keen on riding in the car with him. I would accept the ride on discharge though. I woke last night in a sweat.

Tuesday afternoon. An extraordinary group. A young man named Abdul spoke eloquently and I was stirred to respond. I feel I could begin to read fiction now. I'll ask Sam to bring some of Bellow's novels. Mimi was good enough to try to locate some books while I was on the phone with her today.

WEDNESDAY, MAY 19

I've started reading *Humboldt's Gift*. Charlie Citrine is a wonderful character. I'm filled with hope today for the future. Yesterday I called my office and they told me they'd replaced my office chair with a new one. A very good sign. They're expecting me back.

THURSDAY, MAY 20

I have that raw, scrubbed, newly emergent feeling that comes with being discharged from a mental unit. I feel as though I've been skinned alive with a stiff bristled brush. This morning, clutching all of my belongings in a paper bag they'd given me, I walked out of the hospital and back into my world. Nothing had changed.

Sam had taken duct tape and wrapped it around and around the driver's seat of the car to hold a backrest in place. It looked strange and ugly. He taped a lot of things, the cabinets at home were full of tape, all different kinds. I suppose he felt he couldn't hold things together any longer. Or maybe, and I knew this was closer to the truth of it—maybe he wanted to restrain or bind the object as if by the very act of taping it, he could forever bring together what would by its nature separate or even simply fall apart with time. To hold it very still, very secure, but completely inert—that was why he taped things.

Part One

June 12, 1993

Dr. Michel Bernard
554 Canton Avenue
Briarwood, NY 10023

Dear Dr. Bernard,

I'd like to thank you for the concern you showed for me during my recent hospitalization. You were courteous, visited me on a daily basis and proved perceptive and responsive—important qualities in a doctor.

I feel I must, however, clarify my position for you. When I left the hospital two weeks ago, you informed me about the professional courtesy involved in the referral of my case from Dr. Savarino and you gave me a prescription for two weeks of medication. I told you I would call you in a "few weeks." And, good to my word, that's exactly what I did. Although you'd recommended on my discharge papers that I pay a return visit to Dr. Savarino, I made no promise to see him. I do not consider Dr. Savarino my doctor at this time. My reasons are personal. They have nothing to do with either you or Dr. Ciaclos, so you need not worry about that.

During our telephone conversation last week, you strongly advised that I see a psychiatrist or, at the very least, become an outpatient at Mercy's clinic. Maybe if I tell you something about myself, you'll see that my options are somewhat more complicated than the two you've suggested.

Mental illness is extremely episodic in my case, and, considering the stressful life I lead, may just be the normal adjustment to make. In any event, it's been more than 11 years since I was last hospitalized. During that time, I managed very well, with the exception of the tragic death of my oldest daughter, Jane, in 1985.

Shortly after Jane's death, I sought grief counseling for my family and myself. As is wont to happen in families, the others fell away from the counseling and for me, it became a deep soul-searching therapy for five years. For a good part of that time, I was finishing my bachelor's degree and pursuing a master's degree. I paid for therapy and for school from my own pocket. The therapy, with a woman who was a C.S.W., proved to be a deep sounding of my most innermost self in which I explored dreams, childhood fantasies and examined my defense mechanisms. At the end of five years, I left therapy because of pressing financial considerations. I haven't regretted the five years in therapy or the break I made at the end of that time.

But this last episode came out of left field, right out of the blue for me. One minute I was on track, in control of my life, the next I'd completely lost hold of comfortable reality and my own sense of well being. Again, I'd like to thank you for your part in intervention and the long return to wellness. But you can see that for me to seek a psychiatrist's help at this point would needlessly retrace and duplicate what has gone before, while to join Mercy's clinic on my own wouldn't help me to make use of whatever insights emerged from this last episode. Recall that we both agreed that some form of marital counseling would help to resolve the conflicts involved in this episode. But as you pointed out, "your husband doesn't have a problem, because your husband doesn't think he has a problem" a condition of innocence, in my opinion, that serves to excuse his incivility.

All of this to simply explain my dropping from sight for a few weeks! I'm continuing to take the medication you prescribed.

Sincerely,

Jess Hoffman

cc: Dr. Savarino
        Dr. Ciaclos

I'd managed to capture his interest with my letter. He called and asked if I wanted to come and see him. He gave very specific directions to his office. I liked that. He was practicing from an office in the basement of his house. There were scuffmarks on the door to his office, I remember, where his son had kicked it. I imagined the boy must have sensed that something important, something he was not privy to went on behind that door.

I entered by way of a narrow corridor that ran between the garage and the house and then turned down a flight of steps to the basement. Sometimes he left the upstairs door ajar for me and I came down alone to find him at his desk or on the phone. But mostly he ushered me in, accompanied me on the stairs. He had a sort of elegant courtesy toward me--allowing me to descend before him, making sure I was comfortably seated, was it too hot, too cold in the room, a civilized deference, a decorum that asked nothing from me and that I was unused to.

From the times we met in the hospital we were accustomed to having face-to-face discussions either across a table or in chairs opposite each other. This habit had become very important. We met as equals; there was nothing to obstruct. In the office, he had the ubiquitous massive desk and executive chair, but instead he chose to sit directly across from me on a card table chair during our sessions. I was pleased with this arrangement. I felt we'd both been instrumental in deposing the authoritative "I."

August 9, 1993

Dear Dr. Bernard,

You're right, of course. There is only experience and what we make of it. And, if we're fortunate, there are moments of accidental clarity. But what I wanted you to know from the anecdote I told last Saturday was that, at least initially, the result of my "will to self-determination" was a child conceived in pain and borne in shame. Shame. It's a strong word and one that I've been giving a lot of thought in recent days. Shame, and society's identifying mark for it, stigma, and the uses of disguise. What became clearer to me was that the desire to "pre-empt," to be the initiator, to take matters into my own hands, is a very strong response on my part to two situations—when I'm faced with an ambiguous situation for a prolonged period of time and when I'm in a situation where I feel continually helpless or powerless.

Certainly you are correct to say that I only perceive the occurrences and events of my life as extreme; they are, after all, simply part of living, part of the human condition. Still you would deny me the experience of loss. This is risky business, especially when you conclude that since there's no loss, only "exchange," there's no need for grief or lamentation. How can that be? Catastrophe exists. Evil manifests itself. Suffering is palpable. And, like Zora Neale Thurston, I "have been in Sorrow's kitchen and licked out all the pots." I believe that grief and lamentation are, like music and poetry, ways to express the ineffable experience of our lives.

You said, as if it made up for my previous disregard for convention, "but now you are a wife." Yes, that's true, but remember that before I ever became a wife, I was a mother and before I was a mother, I was myself, alone and apart, distinct from all others. I consider wife to be a role, but I consider being a mother inextricably bound up with the process of self realization.

Once again, my friend, everything seems to come back to the question of memory. T.S. Eliot wrote:

This is the use of memory: For liberation—-not less of love but expanding of love beyond desire, and so liberation from the future as well as the past.

I'm still pondering your vivid image of me frozen in time and space. I look forward to our next meeting. I hope your vacation is carefree. I've just finished a wonderful little book called "Cape of Storms" by Andre Brink and now I've begun Simon Schama's account of the French Revolution!

Best regards,
Jess Hoffman

At first we stumbled over differences in language and culture. He'd been educated in Haiti by French Jesuit priests. He spent what little spare time he had listening to French radio and I could tell that at least part of the time, he thought in French or maybe I should say he conceptualized in French. He'd start a sentence in English and then, unable to complete the thought in English, it would come to him, the whole point of the sentence, in French. "Say it in French," I would urge. And when he did, I understood. Like air through a gossamer veil, the meaning came, perhaps because we were both so determined that it should. The whole process of translation fascinated me, made me feel that we were part of something larger and outside ourselves.

That was why I was so taken aback when the misunderstanding occurred. It was my suggestion that I write him a letter during the week or so that he would be on vacation. I thought it would be a good way to stave off any feelings of abandonment I might have. (In actuality, I almost never felt angry or abandoned when a therapist took time off. I considered it to be deserved.) He liked the idea and so I wrote to him as an alternative to the session we missed, never realizing that he assumed that from that time on, a letter would be forthcoming each week. I'd no idea how strong a bond could be forged—how avidly he would read the letters. When I came to our next appointment, he was very agitated. Had I sent him a letter that week? No, I thought the letter was simply to fill in a visit. We'd had our first crisis in confidence.

August 16, 1993

Last evening you touched a nerve. I was stung by your words and rendered mute by them for the rest of the night. There was a time in my life when I feared being unmasked more than anything, but as I grew older and became more introspective, I thought I'd looked behind most of the masks myself. I must admit I didn't think I could be cruel, only resistant.

For my part, I'd like to make some sense from the confusion of thoughts, ideas and emotions that emerged from our session. I realize I can't speak for you, nor can I do anything about the barriers you may have resurrected because I didn't write to you

7

last week as you expected. Will you accept that it was more an act of deferred gratification on my part than an act of resentment toward you?

As long as we're setting ground rules, I'd like you to know that I don't believe a struggle between our consciousnesses on any level will do either of us any good, whether psychological or ideological. I believe the real struggle lies in defying those barriers that prevent our true exchange, an act of connection. You've charged me with never having sought a situation where my reach would exceed my grasp, never having sought a worthy opponent, and, in part, this may be true. (Neither, I might add, did they seek me.) But, while this may be true in particular, it is not true on a philosophical level. I do not accept the label of determinism, although I realize it's a favorite argument used in psychology to defend certain behaviors.

You've offered me an aggressive, intelligent, interactive, corrective therapy. I would ask you for an enthusiastic, rigorous, interactive and perhaps innovative therapy instead. I've lived with aggression for years and I'm weary of protecting my boundaries, of watching my every word and action for its correspondent retribution and punishment. As for a corrective therapy, it implies that all that went before was incorrect, that somehow I've taken the wrong path in the past. I'm not ready to concede that point.

Perhaps a prescriptive therapy is best. Remember that I believe in many levels of consciousness and that nothing is lost on me that's brought to consciousness in the name of personal truth. I can live without your consolation. I've learned the meaning of irreparable, irreplaceable and inconsolable. You see, unlike you, my friend, I don't view life as a zero sum equation, a pie with so many parts, but rather as a proliferation of experiences—the more, the more.

And so, in one sense, you are right, it *is* about "control." But it's also about death, rebirth, new life, the unfamiliar and different, about growth and regression, about categorical fate and wish fulfillment, about small pleasures like holding a week old infant in your arms or the physical freedom of swimming. It's about the anguish of separation and the need for self mastery.

8

Emerson wrote that "a great soul will be strong to live, as well as strong to think." You've done a terrible thing, my perception shaper. You've taken away my appetite for serendipitous reading. Well, maybe I'll write instead until it returns.

I believe we covered a lot of territory in last evening's session. To my own astonishment, I've been very candid with you in a very short time. We only have words to work with, language is our only connection. That's what makes my not writing to you last week such an absolute blunder.

When I spoke about my father, you pressed me for an end to the story. Once again you sought to close the loop, sought resolution, while I sought to leave it open. But if you must have the satisfaction of completion — he is dead. As are all the others. Or lost to me. They can only serve as archetypes—mythical figures. Use them. Use me.

Until Monday, I remain,

Jess Hoffman

Thus, the letters began as a grievous misunderstanding, an error of omission, an omission that clearly demonstrated how what we really mean often eludes or evades the "other" and how words betray as well as reveal our deepest wishes. The letters soon became an important part of my therapy and an aid in my recuperation.

I'd wait a day or so after the session to think about what we'd spoken about and then on Tuesday or Wednesday evening (sometimes both), I'd write the letter. It would always be mailed on Thursday morning from the same post box before I got on the train to go to work, so that he'd receive it in time to think it through before we met again. He told me that he often read my letters several times over.

Having at heart a certain economy, I reasoned that in the past, I'd gone over problems in therapy related to having had a "disaffected" mother, but I hadn't really dealt with an absentee father and all the substitute fathers and what that meant in my life. I told myself that here was the perfect opportunity to hash out the father/daughter thing with a man who in no way threatened me.

But he was ten years younger than me and he had a very ingenuous way about him, so it was difficult not to cast him as a bright ebullient boy and then take the reins of the conversation away from him and turn the hour in any way I fancied. I could see it took a good deal of restraint for him to actually listen to me rather than hear his own voice, his own words during the hour. I doubted he would have the patience for a long-term therapy, something I pictured like knitting or crocheting and then unraveling the yarn, only to knit it up again. I'd be proven right on this point.

August 24, 1993

So, my friend,

I've felt very cheerful the last several days. And clean, as if I were washed clean. Is it because you've treated me with compassion rather than judging me? You've acted like "Hercules spinning at the feet of Oomphale...protecting and virile like the father and at the same time being used as if he were the mother. Man is feminized here, not so much because the woman wants to castrate him but because she wants to be sure of his loving, maternal, reassuring and undangerous role." A quote I've borrowed from one of my papers.

I think that there was a double thread running through our last session; my feeling of lacking provenance and therefore having to invent myself (a secret and internal process), and a precipitous desire to have you in some way define my external boundaries by rendering a "diagnosis." I wanted you to pronounce the "name and weight of the patriarchy" as the French philosophers call it. In essence, I was asking you to redefine me, but by asking so soon, by demanding a diagnosis from you so early in our relationship, I was asking to be imprisoned, captured in a meaningless categorization. My punishment would be your punishment, since I obviously resent your power to make the diagnosis of my particular madness, my fine insanity.

Both threads are inevitably tangled up in my feeling of being "fatherless," of lacking a loving, protecting and consoling father. A man who would recognize me, who when he looked at me would see something of himself, who couldn't look away or withdraw without remembering the inextricable bond between us. As well as the immutable taboos. This last very important.

So you see, it isn't ownership I refer to so much as it is the irrefutable source of my belongingness. Women who have this paternal source seem to be able to navigate the world far better than I can. They achieve more. I'm always afraid to exceed my mother, for fear that there's nothing beyond her maternal presence—a kind of freefall. World without end. Annihilation of the fragile self I've so carefully created from the bits and pieces of a scattered and marginal life. The prospect of failure and regression to the helplessness of infancy looms large.

Maybe because he wasn't there, wasn't a part of the family drama, my father became the most important part of the family drama. Maybe without a father I've consigned myself to a certain singularity of perception, which you've interpreted as being fixed in time and space. Like a butterfly mounted on a pin. I know that relying solely on my imaginative powers has made it difficult for me to discern the difference between solitude and isolation, social ostracism and alienation. Remember that I grew up in a single parent home when it was euphemistically referred to as a "broken home." My mother had no social status whatsoever as a divorcee. She was feared by respectable married women as a woman of loose morals and wild appetites.

Simone de Beauvoir wrote:

> But what can be done without masculine support by a woman for whom man is at once the sole means and the sole reason for being? She is bound to suffer every humiliation; a slave cannot have the sense of human dignity; it is enough if a slave gets out of it with a whole skin.

It was an opening, an opportunity to explore what it's like to be "fatherless." Perhaps neither of us were sure enough to pursue this, but the wish for a loving, protective, consoling man in my life, one who wanted nothing sexual from me stood in stark contrast to all those shadowy figures, phantoms really, who surrounded my mother while I was growing up and the oppressive figure my husband had become.

September 2, 1993

Last evening you asked "do you love him?" Isn't it enough that I once loved him. Too much has happened for me to love him as I once did. Besides, over the years my idea of love changed. Perhaps we moderns love only the myth of "being in love." I only know that what I feel now is closer to allegiance. You see we're inextricably bound by the sheer horror of having looked into each other's eyes as we stood peering into the abyss, stood on either side of our daughter's grave. And what we saw there cannot be expressed. It seemed then that our only choice was just to survive. But then, to my surprise, life offered more choices. So I took what was left of me and I grew and changed, even thrived.

You asked why I don't leave him. Sometimes I think I've spent these last eight years doing nothing else. Do I really need to actually leave him in order to be alone? I'm more alone *with* him. After all, he rarely shows me mercy or tolerance these days. He doesn't support me, nurture or encourage me. And although he desires me, he struggles to make love to me. He can only disappoint me, since I insist on remembering what he used to be like. Maybe this is what Eliot meant by "love beyond desire."

Anger takes on a life of its own, or it divorces itself from life in the service of death dealing, or life denying, or the compulsion to make someone's life unendurable simply for the sake of doing it, simply because it has become the shape of the angry one's life to punish.

The habit of punishment is quickly acquired and self-supporting. It has one food, plentiful and easily obtained: the need for blame. In this, it is a really very comprehensible attempt to render a senseless universe sensible. Everything that is, particularly everything that one wishes were otherwise, must have its cause, and so its causer. Perhaps the person taken over by deadly anger is for this reason, at bottom, pitiable , like Dostoyevsky's Grand Inquisitor, who demanded death on a large scale so that suffering could be reduced.

Mary Gordon, *Newsday*, June 13, 1993

You've accused me of not having the courage to leave him. How do you know it is not more courageous to stay...remember, I've left a man before. I know what one must do and how to do it. Personal courage is not discernible to others. I've always believed that each of us knows down deep what takes the most courage, which path is more difficult. I only know that I no longer love power for itself, yet I cannot abide powerlessness—that I love life and defy death—that I will stay with him, but I will never again follow him.

You've given me yet another book to read, my intelligent young doctor! And I've only just ordered the last book from the library—the Dumas novel. Isn't it enough that you've invaded my private domain through these letters. Must you now dictate what has been up until now a delightfully haphazard reading list guided only by my own interest and desire?

Best regards,

Jess Hoffman

I was becoming quite a francophile, looking for ways into his life even as he probed my mind. I wanted to acquire the language, but not enough to learn it in any legitimate way. I bought a French-English dictionary and looked for phrases to use in the letters.

By now we'd agreed more or less on the ground rules and he was becoming increasingly more confrontational as he grew surer of me. I could tell he wanted me to fit into an idealized patient category, a patient of whom he could be proud, perhaps boast of his effect upon me at some later time. He said he'd found the technique of modeling quite effective with his patients. I felt we were too different. My aim was for him to at least have to speak from the standpoint of an informed inquisitor.

He hadn't brought up the contents of any of my letters at our sessions. I was beginning to feel as if the letters were our "dirty little secret," as if they belonged to some dark corner of his basement where we furtively groped each other like children and whispered, "don't tell, never tell." I resolved to speak about this to him at our next session.

September 15, 1993

Cher beau frere,

> In the end, the changed life for women will be marked, I feel certain, by laughter...And with laughter comes the end of fantasy and daydreaming...Women... who found their way to a meaningful life identified daydreaming as a sign of their meaningless lives and the only consolation for them.. The acceptance of a new challenge in middle or old age marks the end of fantasy, and the substitution...work. It marks also the end of the dream closure.
>
> *Writing a Woman's Life*
> Carolyn Heilbrun

Just because I made you laugh at our last session, I don't want you to think that my life is like an opera buffo! And please don't construe my relationship with Sam as simply role reversal. It does an injustice to your fine mind to oversimplify my situation in that way. Role reversal, aside from being a superficial arrangement, implies that two people consciously and willingly trade places for the purpose of mutual satisfaction or for some gain. If anything, our roles have been blurred by age and circumstance, not consciously and effectively reversed. We haven't even a strategy for effectively coping with life's lesser problems. And quite frankly, I should like to live without roles for the rest of my life.

What I've been trying to do "purposefully" in the last eight years has nothing to do with assuming a masculine role. I'm interested in becoming "fully human." Sam is cynical and disillusioned, childish, bitter. He'd rather remain unhappy than adapt or try to make something of his life. You see if he tries, there's always the risk he will fail. No, you're wrong—we don't perceive Sam as "feminized." He isn't reassuring and maternal or nurturing. There's always the ever-present threat of rage lurking just beneath his surface. This is how he emotionally manages us. We, on the other hand, are not permitted to be angry—we must remain easy and cheerful. As Carolyn Heilbrun wrote: "If one is not permitted to express anger or even recognize it within oneself, one is, by simple extension, refused both power and control."

I don't know what you mean when you say I have too much "purpose." I only want to protect myself against my own fantasies. You see, the more real you become for me, the less I will indulge in fantasies about you, the less I will be held in thrall, the less I will seek the comfort of the couch. Is it so wrong to seek mastery over myself? After all, I do not seek to dominate you. Only to know you as a real person. It helped to learn that you love opera as much as I do, for instance.

The letters, I fear, will lead to an unhealthy narcissism—not a good narcissism where I love myself before I love the other, but a narcissistic construction in which I am both myself and the other. In the letters, you are whoever I want you to be. Father, brother, lover, friend. Our actual friendship cannot yet sustain the content of the letters. Especially since, as I pointed out at our last session, they lie between us unanswered, unacknowledged, a shared secret. While it's true I'm able to clarify my thinking on

15

certain points we touch on in actual meetings and perhaps provide you with additional insights in the letters, I still wonder if we're not substituting one bad habit for another. Are we deceiving ourselves, mon cher?

Here is another of the things Heilbrun says in what is one of my favorite books:

> The true representation of power is not of a big man beating a smaller man or a woman. Power is the ability to take one's place in whatever discourse is essential to action and the right to have one's part matter. This is true in the Pentagon, in marriage, in friendship, and in politics.

But I digress...as I'm wont to do in these letters that I shoot into the air!

I have eight operas on my subscription to the Met this season. Tosca is the first on October 2, and Placido Domingo will sing. I'm very much looking forward to it.

Next Monday seems far away. Today at sundown marks the beginning of the Jewish high holy days. To you and yours I wish the year to be as full and round as a challah bread. L'Shana Tova! Happy New Year, my friend.

Jess Hoffman

Of course he'd claimed that even though he hadn't responded specifically to my letters, we were actually talking about the letters at all of our sessions. In some oblique way the letters informed our conversations, shaped the dialogue between us. Still, the particulars didn't seem to matter to him. In fact, he told me he was listening to me to better identify the larger themes and motifs in what I told him. That he was trained to do this. I, on the other hand, had only my instincts to rely on. I was used to watching, to listening for the least little change in the timbre of the voice, for the telling expression or the gesture that gave meaning to the talk.

Early on in the hospital, he'd asked me whether I was a "literary woman," and I'd said that I was. I immediately regretted characterizing myself in this way. After all, a mental ward is a great equalizer, everything is geared toward sameness and normalcy, to people blending in and submitting to round after round of self-help exercises based on our all having the same needs and inclinations.

September 22, 1993

Pour l'homme noir,

Clearly, you feel free to change the rules in the middle of the game. It's a very professional and worthwhile endeavor for you to seek the underlying or overweening themes in our talks, one that applies to modern literary criticism as well. Virginia Woolf wrote that one should always seek, in reading, to locate that certain blind spot at the back of the author's head. So, my good doctor, I believe it's right that you should seek the theme in what I tell you of my story and not be mislead by the words. But it hardly seems fair for you to criticize the style in which I tell you my story! You find me "self deprecating!" Perhaps it's modesty on my part. Or perhaps I'm humble. Maybe I'm more keenly aware of my categorical fate than you. Or more willing to castigate myself for my own acts and deeds. In short, perhaps it's evidence of a healthy, working conscience, which you mistake for self-deprecation. At least I'm willing to take responsibility for myself. For every person doing exactly what they please in this world, I guarantee you will find two in chains.

I thought we were attempting a dialogue. It's an art, this quest for themes, or so you told me a few sessions ago. Is it only an art for you? Is it instead a school examination for me, one in which I've failed in "self image?" You told me, when we began, that the one unforgivable sin would be to withhold some part of my story from you, but when I attempt to be completely candid with you, you pay little attention to content and address only my style. My friend, I also search for themes.

17

I doubt I will ever be able to make you understand. Somehow, you've come to view me as this uptight white woman, who, if she only learned how to relax, would be able to throw away her metaphorical crutches and dance and sing in the sunlight. Well, aside from the fact that my soul only dances beneath the moon, I've suffered more crashing disappointments, setbacks, disruptions, more of life's surprises, than most of the people I know. It's a wonder I even function at all, given my history and genetic predisposition. Yet, this is me. And that, my friend, is the point. Even the crutches are me. Perhaps, the most important part of me, for I've fashioned them myself. Once naked, I've managed to pull the tattered cloth of decency around me. Not respectability, I have no use for it. But common decency.

Don't confuse my restraint with frigidity. I'm passionately disposed to live this life until that time when I will be reunited with my daughter. Yes, you're right, we *are* all actors, but some of us have roles that matter more than others. I would very much like mine to matter.

As for my mother—she had little pride or self-respect. Her self-loathing got the best of her and it became easier for her to sink to degradation than to lift her skirts and walk to higher ground. I was simply baggage to her. Did I envy her? I only know that I needed her desperately and she wasn't there for me. I was not held precious.

My mother lacked character, imagination and integrity. To her credit, she showed enormous determination, individualism and great physical courage. Because she lacked imagination, she was neither intuitive, sensitive, sensual or passionate. Because I possessed imagination, I invented a mother who possessed these qualities and then loved her with all the fervency of a child until well into adulthood. How could I not? She was the only parent I had.

In actuality, she was a nasty, craven woman who systematically undertook to alienate all those who were close to her. But above all else, she was nothing without a man. An independent woman? No, I think not. She was an unambiguous woman. But enough of her. It's really too painful.

I think I've come full circle in this letter, because suddenly I see a theme. You're right, I've styled myself a spectator before life. I'd much rather observe than participate—and from a comfortable sideline—obscurity. Am I so precious to you, cher ami, that you'd like me to live long like your ingenuous uncle who didn't know what day it was? I thank you for the prescription. But I must always know what day it is. And I'm sure that any mother in Jeremie knew that October 1 was the first day of school. That's part of our job. Even as a secretary, I must know what day it is and where he should be at every hour. To be a shadow. That's my value. I'm thinking about my breathing, as you suggested, until Monday.

Jess Hoffman
The Reading Woman

He'd been reading Alexander Dumas' classic *La Belle Dame aux Camellias*. I don't think he was aware of how romanticized a notion it was of "the fallen woman," the woman cast out from respectable society, inevitably paying the ultimate price, death, for her indiscretions. I knew, of course, because of my mother's sad and wasted life, that real life "bad girls," unlike their fictional counterparts weren't cast off, only made to live on the margin of society and that they didn't die for their sins, but lived a shadowy and indistinct existence of insult and injury -- nights of bargain and abandon -- empty days. Still something like a long-lost sympathy for the reprobate and disreputable was kindled in me by his romantic notions.

Although initially it seemed as if we were in agreement philosophically, it soon became apparent to me that he and I were at different ends of the spectrum. Mostly we argued about the past, present and future. He was, I felt, nihilistic, insisting that those who lived only in the present were the healthiest among us in both mind and body. Since my daughter's death, I had only the past, only memory for succor. For me to be out of touch with what was going on around me, to be free of my past, would be a mortal sin.

September 29, 1993

Dear kindly interrogator,

I can read your face, you know. I know when you lower your eyes and make that little moue with your mouth that you've understood and can tolerate what I'm telling you—that somewhere inside, you've granted me clemency. And sometimes I see the pupils of your eyes get huge and dark and I know that you're feeling some powerful emotion, or I see just a flicker of a smile in your eyes while I'm talking and then it runs across your lips and I know that I've said something to amuse you. Yes, I can read your face.

You asked me if I thought I was unique. I know my problems are not unique and I know there is nothing new under the sun, but doesn't your question belie a form of psychological reductionism? And your insistence that all roles are of equal importance, isn't that also reductionism as well? I'd hoped that we might have a unique discourse, one in which neither of us seeks to dominate the other or seeks consensus at the lowest common denominator. After all, we're so wonderfully different. Why not celebrate what I am that you are not and vice versa. You see, I know I'm passionate about life because I still possess enthusiasm and curiosity. J'avais desir. I thought that perhaps our talks might lead to heightened consciousness for both of us. That's what I think "living" is, after all. A kind of heightened awareness of yourself and others, a sentient awareness. And madness is the foe of all of that, a place to be seriously avoided at all costs.

I think that when I spoke about not being able to read or to write my name when I was in hospital that was what I wanted you to know. I see no contradiction in terms when I speak of that heightened consciousness as being finite. Beyond death, my soul, I hope, will be bound up with all the others. There's time enough for sameness, eternity is sameness. Now is for "differance."

You know, I was a very charming child. One of the first things I knew about myself was that I had this power to attract—

20

if I smiled at people, they smiled back at me. I can remember holding my mother's hand and testing this out when we walked along a street. I smiled at people and they responded. My mother lectured me not to smile at strangers, but I was fascinated by this phenomenon. How did I ever get from that innocent trust to this lonely and alienated place?

I think I've found another strand, another theme, in this tangled web of emotion. During my first hospital stay, Dr. Ciaclos sensed that I was profoundly alienated. Like an absentminded professor, I sometimes forget to connect with other people and, left to my own devices, I eventually withdraw altogether, not realizing the amazingly healthful properties, the lubrication of social relationships. Ciaclos advised me to start making friends, start entertaining at home. In fact, he said, begin immediately by making friends in the hospital. I remember being impressed by that prescription and a little surprised by its simplicity. How did he know I felt so alone when at the time he interviewed me my family surrounded me? I don't know. He just knew. And that, I think, is a part of what I was trying to tell you at our last session. That abject loneliness can overtake me even when I'm among other people.

Is this letter long enough? You make me feel as if I'm a coward for putting my thoughts down like this. Am I deflecting emotion by the act of writing? Sometimes in the letters it's easier to be angry with you or indignant or to rail against some stereotypical conclusion I believe you've drawn about me. I suppose I need a course in the art of confrontation, but I'd much rather entertain a grand literary salon. I've enclosed a poem by Ezra Pound about a lady who entertained one of the most famous salons in London. Although Pound was being terribly cynical about her, he inadvertently uncovered a truth about what makes up a woman's life when she's forced to live vicariously. See if you like it.

I'm thinking about complicity and also about patriarchal bargains, until Monday.

Jess Hoffman

October 5, 1993

Cher ebon ami,

Well, you certainly were blessed with wonderful weather for your vacation. These last several days have been extraordinarily pleasant. I hope it was a carefree time for you. As for me, Saturday's opera was the high point of the week. It left me with a rush of thoughts and feelings.

I suppose I'm energized by the autumn weather, but I absolutely hunger for a sense of productivity in my life, some tangible meaning that I can tally up at the end of the day. I yearn for purposeful acts and deeds, for meaningful work, and for the opportunity to develop a central, adult self. I'm reading a book that says that women have internalized so much of what represses and oppresses us. I feel I've learned this lesson too well—and that's my complicity. I'm the instrument of my own oppression in many instances. But, as usual, I take too much upon myself.

I'm sending you a piece by Anna Quindlen on "voice." Feminists talk about voice quite a lot. I wonder if you're learning anything at all from these letters I send you. I know that I'm learning from you about commitment and dedication. And about innocence and delight—the two somehow go together in your case. Of course, your optimism makes me feel about a thousand years old.

I'm not going to write you a very long letter this week, my friend, since you managed to escape me face to face. By the time we meet again, I will have run away a little myself. Sam and I may go upstate for an overnight this weekend. We'll drive all over the countryside searching out little treasures and the spoils of the autumn harvest. Jusqu'a Lundi, je suis pensee de l'autumn et de l'optimisme. (My conjugations are disgraceful, aren't they?)

Jess

I'd condemned him for being a poor listener during our sessions, but I had to admit that he was an avid and interested reader. I was beginning to enjoy the idea that my letters had such a singularly passionate audience. At the end of each session, he would walk upstairs with me, all the while enjoining me to write an even longer letter the next week. Or he'd suggest that I write the letters in longhand or even record them so he could listen to them. And every week he'd suggest a different cure, a positive prescription for living that he'd tell me as we parted. They were innocuous enough -- breathing exercises, meditation, a list of pros and cons for making decisions -- the usual self-help, self-improvement homework.

When I told him that I'd put off asking for a raise at work, he suggested that I write out the request and read it aloud to him the following week. "I know people like you," he said, "who ask for nothing and then one day they just don't show up at all." And although I balked at his request, I finally acquiesced.

October 13, 1994

Part I

Preface to an onerous task

There are several reasons why I find the task you set for me this week distasteful. The main one, I suppose, is that I believe hindsight to be unproductive. I feel as if I'm being coerced for the sake of the "therapeutic process" to recant what I view as a perfectly legitimate exercise of my own good judgement in order to confirm your analysis of a situation in which you are a third party! It goes against my grain to reconstruct a face to face conversation during which I felt emotionally confident, intuitively and spontaneously in sync, in order to paint a more psychologically prophylactic picture of myself for you, one that must answer the all-pervasive "poor self image" indictment. Besides, to speak the words I would speak to one person to another seems to me to be duplicitous and contrived.

Having said that, I should also let you know that I resent your accusation that I fear the truth. I may harbor fears and insecurities (I have freely written to you along these lines), but the "truth" doesn't belong to me or to you or to my boss, in this case; it's something we must arrive at together. If I were subject to performance reviews at work, we might be better able to discuss my professional worth, but I'm not—I'm worth what is tacitly agreed upon by myself and my boss and that's never based on what I did for him yesterday, but what I'm doing for him today and may do for him tomorrow. I felt that I confronted this issue realistically with him, even though I knew that he may not have given a second thought to my request for a raise. You think otherwise.

Lastly, you dismissed the importance of my discussing the issue of my raise with my friends. Only last week I wrote to you about a tendency to allow myself to drift from relationships! My friends provide an all important support network on which I rely. They are quick to offer solace and slow to criticize. I never underestimate the importance of forming and maintaining friendships-it's part of the cure for my particular madness. Besides, friendship is pleasurable! And that brings me to my final topic: your advice to read less and "act" more. All of my actions are predicated on being "suspended in language." Without the pleasure of reading, I would be infinitely less prepared to decode this world. I've told you that my reading is an "acceptable escape," and that my only guide is interest and desire. Pleasure. What D.W. Winnicott referred to as that "potential space." "Here where there is trust and reliability is a potential space," he wrote, "one that can become an infinite area of separation which the baby, child, adolescent, adult may creatively fill with playing, which in time becomes the enjoyment of the cultural heritage." Winnicott claimed that the fashioning of this potential space is part of what makes life worth living. No, my friend, don't ask me to give up my books. You might as well ask me to give up on life. For, if I believe in anything, it's the preeminence of language. Without it, we could not even have psychiatry.

Part II - The onerous task

For a while I'd anticipated that my annual raise which is really a cost of living adjustment, might reflect the difference I perceive in my work since you came on board last January. Perhaps, I thought, there will be some recognition of my having been instrumental in the smooth and orderly transfer of power in April from the old authoritarian style of your predecessor to a more inclusive and progressive leadership under your good instincts. However, I didn't give you to understand my expectations. I'm not even sure how the subject of my raise was presented to you by the office manager. I have a hunch, however, that it was not framed as a matter of "how much," so much as it was "should she receive it or not." I realize that you've been President less than a year and have, in that time, instituted many changes in the dynamics of the office; the biggest change being the "humanizing" of what was formerly a severely alienated staff. I also know that several people have resisted and continue to resist that change. I have welcomed the change and tried to facilitate it as much as possible. But we're all inured to the old ways. When I asked about my annual raise, I asked from an uncomfortable and childlike position, like Oliver Twist asking for more food. "Please, sir, may I have some more?" And you assured me as if placating a child. It makes sense that if the request was made in a childlike manner, the reply would attempt to appease the child, would be paternalistic in nature. But when I decided to approach you in future, I also decided that I wouldn't come to you like a good little girl for the requisite pat on the head. I would come to you as a woman with expertise and longtime experience, prepared to back up my request with documented performance. This week I asked to attend a staff meeting that was, in my opinion, important to my work. You agreed that I should attend and even recommended I attend a follow up meeting at which you weren't present. This indicates a beginning step toward making my position as your secretary more productive and meaningful. With the development of my position, I'll be able to ask for compensation based on performance, not for those shadowy and unspoken functions that inevitably lie between master and slave.

I believe that we will reach some mutually satisfying agreement if I'm properly prepared and we have enough trust in each other. For now, it's too soon, you're still new, still too dependent on me and others in the office to act deliberately. But in six months, we will have taken each other's measure. You'll have tamed your Board of Directors and built a team of your staff. It's been a long time since I felt a man had to not only anticipate my every wish, but also grant it. Recognition at this point is only a wish—in the future, I'll base my request for a raise and the amount of that raise on more than my wish for recognition.

Of course, I haven't mentioned my having left you decidedly vulnerable in May. Just at the time when you were beginning to trust my judgment, I "break down." Nevertheless, you spoke candidly with me on my return, and I'm doing everything in my power to prevent any more episodes of that nature from happening. The real question, I suppose, is have I forgiven myself for that episode. Perhaps not. Perhaps I don't feel I deserve reward or recognition at this point. That my absence for three weeks in May was like a minus sign in the negative column that I have to work toward erasing. Still, I didn't simply thank you for the standard annual raise. I told you I felt that I must come knocking at your door again in the future. That means I'm not resigned to my fate. And you said you'd be there when I knocked.

Part III - Some follow-up thoughts to the onerous task

Cher ebon ami,

What a struggle this was for me! And how it brought up old baggage! Perhaps we are all actors, but surely there must be a provident place in each of our lives, where we can be ourselves, plain and simple. It's not your duty to search for my voice, it's my struggle to find it. And when I find it, it must be distinct from your voice. You do me no favor asking me to play roles—

26

it's in casting off roles that I'll finally find my true voice. My employer does not pay for my voice. He pays only for my time.

You know, my friend, it occurs to me that therapy with a man is like going to Elizabeth Arden for the "Red Door Treatment." There's a necessary tearing down of all you are so that you can be remade, and then it's in his image! With a woman therapist, it doesn't matter how long it takes, or how much she must disregard, she will inevitably find some good in you just as you are.

I really liked it, I must admit, when last week you referred to my "professional" life and indirectly to my "personal" life. You understand the duality of public and private.

Ah, well, shall we continue?

Jess

Strange how this exercise in artifice had served to set the scene for one of our most candid sessions. For the first and only time, he'd chosen to sit behind his big desk. I, in my most insouciant manner, leaned casually on the desk to read the text, for the first time a letter read in his presence, a letter as part of the therapy, my thoughts on paper read aloud in the white light of his office. It had an exhilarating, liberating effect on me. He had ascended to a position of authority, but I'd transcended the entire situation, wrapping him in my words, using the stratagem most familiar to me of all feminine strategies, la langue, to cajole, to persuade, to appease, to encompass. I found my triumph in surrender, my honesty in pretense, my pride, my joy in the wordless boundary of words. For the first time, I felt a real connection.

Wednesday, October 20, 1993

Cher ebon ami,

Isn't it funny how having your desk between us seemed to have brought down emotional barriers? Well, walls continue to tumble for me in a rush of associations and I can only attribute it to our last session. Maybe it had something to do with our restoring you to your rightful place as doctor, myself as your patient, or maybe it had to do with Winnicott's "potential space" where trust and reliability enable separation. Or, it could be the ten minutes you so generously bestowed on me at the end of the hour. Mostly though, it was your pressing me for an answer about last week's onerous task: "why did you do it?" I think I did it to prove to you that I wasn't afraid of the truth. Because the truth was in what I read to you. I just had to find it for myself. I wanted to prove that I was courageous and my own soul. Anyway, let me see if I can describe this to you as it occurred to me this morning.

I woke from a very deep sleep in which I dreamt that I was urinating and the loss of control was a great feeling of release. As you know, I almost died from a peritoneal infection when I was a child and there was an episode in the hospital of mistreatment and severe deprivation. My childish perception was that my mother had abandoned me. When I was brought to the hospital, I was running a high fever and was dehydrated, according to my mother's account. During the hospital stay I became incontinent, at an age when I was probably just beginning to achieve control of my bladder. Our family doctor was away, and according to my mother, I received little or no care during his absence. Supposedly only upon his return was I properly looked after? But the nurses reported to my mother that I was pining away for her, wouldn't eat. My actual memory of this time is limited only to a scene where my mother is walking away from my crib toward an elevator, getting into the elevator and I'm screaming for her, but the elevator doors close and she is gone. I'm alone. I have a stuffed animal, a horse, with me and I hold on to it. Subsequently, I would have "accidents" at school lasting into the third and fourth grades. My mother sent a note to school asking that I be allowed to use the bathroom when it was necessary without waiting for permission. I was, of course, mortified by my incontinence.

I woke from the dream—ordinarily I would have lost control in reality, but I hadn't. I kept hearing you say, "why did you do it?" I was thinking about my father. About pleasing him. About pleasing you. Where was he during the time I was in the hospital as a child? I have absolutely no recall of him during that time. But I suspect that right around that age, I was beginning to have romantic feelings towards him. All the pain and the shame were mixed up with the pleasure of release. Of letting go. And always the terror and anger of abandonment followed by the determination to survive. Defiance.

We must have forged new paths in my psyche the other evening, because all day today I've been overwhelmed by recollections and disjointed scenes from the past. It occurs to me that with the desk between us, we became more intimate. Strange, but I value the inherent contradiction. Perhaps if you had not dared, if I had not risked the onerous task. There is something to be said for conflict and confrontation. And as usual, I know someone who said it!

Jean Baker Miller, in her book, *Toward A New Psychology of Women,* wrote that women must reclaim conflict since it is "inevitable, the source of all growth and an absolute necessity if one is to be alive…women's present ability to recognize the necessity for conflict if they are to pursue their self-defined self-interest can therefore be a first, great primary source of strength." Of course, reclaiming conflict means risk and according to Baker Miller, "risk, in its psychic meaning and impact becomes the risk of abandonment and condemnation."

Well, mon medecin bon, you certainly have me doing my homework! I'm thinking about conflict and about valor, jusqu'a Lundi. Bonne nuit.

Jess

Thursday, October 28, 1993

Cher ebon ami,

What a week! I'm exhausted, but it's a good exhaustion. So much has been happening. Psychologically, the walls continue

29

to fall for me. I had a dream Monday evening after our session. I've been working late at the office practically every evening this week except when I've been at my friend Lenny's house working with him on concert programs and concert tickets. When I work with Lenny, the work is fairly straightforward and so I have no problems with it. In fact, I'm feeling fortunate to have three "amiable" men with good dispositions playing large roles in my life right now—you, Lenny, and my boss. My most anxious moments, as it turned out this week, were because the LIRR was stalled several times on the homebound trip.

But, I digress from the dream: I dreamt I was visiting the home of a childhood playmate. Betty was also a child of divorce and I suppose we gravitated toward each other. When we were about 8 years old, we would play at being grownups, mothers to our dolls, wives with imaginary husbands. Later, during our pre-teen years, we indulged each other for a period of time as substitutes for boys, a lot of homoerotic petting and fondling. But in the dream, Betty had become a very wealthy and successful woman — her home was like a theme park with elaborate gardens and water displays. She had a baby boy, and for some reason, in the dream I was carrying him in order to give him back to her. While I carried him I bathed him in a series of baths, waterfalls and showers that I made my way through in her house. Another woman accompanied me, but I don't know who it was. We finally found Betty at a sort of restaurant bar. But when I saw the woman behind the counter, it wasn't Betty at all.

I haven't thought about Betty for a very long time nor have I seen her for many years. She was not the friend that I idealized or aspired to be like. That was someone else. Still, in some ways we did console each other as children.

So my friend, it seems as if we have begun the long task of defining ourselves, you and I. I've learned that as a mother, you make a very good father and that although we are both "suspended in language," for you it's the aural aspect that is most important, the word that's heard, and I'm more visual, the written word attracts me most.

Because you gave me the prescription and your beeper number (even though it proved to be the wrong number!), I felt as if I had a bodyguard everywhere I went and in every situation this week. And the imaginary bodyguard was in contrast to the extraordinary sense I had all week of my own vulnerability. It was as if I lived in the very center of a paradox—and my vulnerabilities became my strengths. I'm grateful to you, mon medecin. Not only are you intelligent and alert, but you're fully prepared to protect me from myself when necessary. I like that.

Well, the rush is just about over at my office and tonight there's a feeling of lassitude, much like I would have after I took final exams in school. I have a sense of time well spent, important activity, accomplishment. Tonight I'll sleep a sleep I earned. Tomorrow is my birthday. My inclination is to spend the weekend incognito reading a book. And then perhaps on Sunday, I'll visit Jane's grave for the last time until spring. It is too heartbreaking to go during the winter. I sometimes wonder if Jane would recognize me now. I've changed so since she died. Dear friend, I'm so deep in this therapeutic process so quickly and so freely I can hardly believe it. Je vous remercie de votre aide. Jusqu'a Lundi,

Jess

At the time, I was working two jobs, a strategy that I'd employed since my daughter's death and even before to escape or create alternate routes of escape from certain untenable life situations. It was a lot easier than just quitting a job. I'd done that too. Starting with my divorce in 1968, there had been a series of "quitting the job" experiences. It seemed the only way I could take charge of my life. I found that quitting, much like divorce, required a particular kind of courage -- not endurance, I had that -- but the courage to act assertively on one's own behalf. And that generally robbed me of what little emotional resources I'd stockpiled. Quitting a job, like leaving a man, required a show of self-confidence that I seldom felt. Quitting was stepping down, dropping out, and giving up a self in order to regroup and reinvent one. It was a long, slow process of reordering that needed to take place.

But working several jobs at the same time, layering myself according to what was necessary, adapting my self to different and various situations, that was right up my alley. I'd been doing that all my life. So from 9 to 5, I worked at traditional jobs, supporting and serving others, anticipating their needs, doing tasks created for me, not by me. After hours, however, I was the employer. I'd worked up a small editorial design business. We did, my friend Lennie and I, resumes, promotional materials, business letters and forms, newsletters and all sorts of small desktop jobs. Like my marriage, my work life reflected my basic problem. One was not enough and two was often too many.

Wednesday evening, November 3, 1993

Cher ebon ami,

The city grows very gray with the change in daylight and I'm winding down from the exhilaration of meaningful work last week. I cannot believe that with your quick mind you had difficulty getting through school. Emerson said on the subject of scholarship: "Truly speaking, it is not instruction, but provocation, that I can receive from another soul."

I think several themes run through our last several sessions: change, difference and courage. My courage flags in the face of a challenge. I turn to you and use you as the object with which I bridge the abyss. You are like the stuffed animal, the horse I held tight to in the hospital during that terrible time of abandonment and physical disintegration.

Ah, but do I sense a gentle probe, the precision of a diagnostic instrument introduced at our last session? Would you really want to perform an e.g. on me — probe my brain to find the exact nature of its synapses, measure the units of excitation, the "qms", and follow the intricate breaching, the "bahnung" in order to effect a miraculous cure? Surely it's not as simple as that. I'm a complicated personality, and aside from the label of "social engineering" that comes to mind, there are other reasons why you can't perform a quick fix with me, however seductive

32

the idea may be to you. For one thing, as I told you, I don't faint, nor do I black out. That seems to me to be intellectually irresponsible. The body may quicken or weaken according to circumstance, but the only time I've been unconscious was when sodium pentothal was administered during a minor procedure, a tubal ligation ten years ago, or during the delivery of the afterbirth of my children. "Seizures" suggests itself to me in terms of religious ecstasies, which we were talking about in our last session. Even during orgasm, the closest thing I can think of to a seizure, I don't "black out." No, my friend, I don't think the problem, if it is a problem, is "inter-ectal," so much as it is an inability on my part to affirm my "entelechy."

I think the real question here is why you wish to do this thing. It strikes me that I was describing my objectification by Sam the week before — where every act of free agency or assertiveness on my part has an immediate and corresponding repressive response from him. Is it because I no longer sit in the patient's chair? Have I displaced you? I'm only seeking a different perspective. Or perhaps the suggestion to look into my brain is a creative one on your part. As Pygmalion, you will make me perfect. It seems curious. And painfully reminiscent of my premature and importunate request for a diagnosis. What I'm hoping for from this therapy is a whole self, a way to integrate what seems at times to be disparate parts of myself. I would hope that between us, we could conjure up this whole self. For you to suddenly introduce the idea of a biological determination startles me. Have you no patience for discovery?

Still, I'm beginning to see a reflection of myself in you, self as a prisoner, an inert self emerges, a self that is fearful of disintegrating in the normal commotion and interactions of daily life. Are you intentionally mirroring cet personne?

Cher psychologue, this letter seems long and without any center. I think that was what I was hoping our friendship would be like...that we would suggest ourselves to ourselves and define our actual differences without closure. But now I see that you are ambitious to cure me. Jusqu'a Lundi, I remain

Moi-meme, sain et sauf

Jess

Always with increased intimacy would come the wish to bring a gift -- to give something, to further reveal persona and in so doing, to have increased the other's measure. Was all of this to simply say, "I'm a writer?" -- was it such an outrageous statement on my part that my very sanity came into question? And if I was a writer, was I writing my life in this dialogue?

I'd brought him a bound copy of my thesis. How slavishly devoted I'd been to scholarly language when I wrote it. It was stiff and academic, but at the time, I remember feeling that I'd said all I wanted to say, something I'd never been able to claim before and that women were always being kidded about not being able to do. And at the time I felt as if the stakes had never been higher. I knew that he would never read it with the passion to know me that would equal my passion to be known. Nevertheless, he took it from me without even asking if I was giving it or lending it. It belonged to him.

Wednesday evening, November 11, 1993

Cher ebon ami,

I used a very appropriate metaphor the other evening. If you recall, I said that this therapy was like an underground river for me and I felt that it had a very vital quality to it. I think what I wanted you to know was how revitalized I feel in this dialogue with you. Because we engaged each other so directly during this last session, mind to mind, so to speak, I find myself with bundles and bundles of things to tell you. Let me see if I can sort through these packages and put them in some sort of order.

Firstly, my bringing you my thesis was not a planned thing. I'd wanted to show it to you — as an object — to entice you to read it, but I dismissed that as an attempt to dominate your time, to burden you with my groping and grasping for meaning. Advertisements for myself. Then, at the last minute, before leaving for your office, I grabbed it and put it in my bag. You needn't read it, you know, now or ever. It's just that lately I've had this strong impulse to show you things — to provide you visual images as shortcuts for words. Anyway, it's done. The gesture is probably worth more than the reading. Actually, I'd intended bringing you something quite different last evening. A sort of written road map of the process of decision making that a close personal friend had shared with me a few evenings ago while we were working on her resume. I found it to be quite extraordinary in its clarity of thought and deliberateness. I thought it would please you. But, it wasn't mine. I brought instead my muddled attempt at making sense of an almost indescribable quality, ecstasy. You see I'm driven by an ego after all!

I have been thinking about what you said about Sam and me, our relationship. Here is the paradox of it. In his possessive, co-optive way, Sam has loved me very well. Having been held in the circle of his love, I was able to grow. Unable to anticipate the direction I would take, Sam attempted to contain my growth. When he couldn't contain it, he punished me and fled himself. I continue to grow. But I do not love my persecutor! That is part of what I've learned in growing up.

I'm going to have to think about your interpretation of Sam as my "enabler." It's an inversion of the role psychology attributes to relatives of alcoholics. And, of course, I'm intrigued by the inversion (as you might suspect I would be) since it reverses the meaning of empowerment. In the conventional interpretation, the "enabler" gives tacit permission or is complicit in a destructive behavior. In your interpretation, Sam, by giving up power has empowered me in a constructive behavior. Am I reading you correctly? That by virtue of the fact that Sam has abdicated his position as head of the household, he's responsible for my taking on additional dimensions of selfhood? Responsible for my individuation and growth? That only when he stands down can I assume a standpoint? Am I then fashioned from Adam's rib, breathing out and in only when he exhales?

Let me digress for a moment. I want to tell you about my island. For undoubtedly I will be thinking about this during my vacation, since solitude presents an appropriate time to work through private feelings and dissolve my feelings of anger and disillusionment.

This will be my fourth or fifth trip. I only go there with GM, my ex-mother-in-law. The reasons that I enjoy my island among all the islands in the Caribbean to which I might travel and the reason I continue to return are these: my island has the good fortune to be located just at that spot where tradewinds converge. Therefore my island enjoys the most temperate of climates. There's always a breeze there, and so, because of this ceaseless motion, I'm never bored. On the other hand, and because nothing is ever entirely one thing, my island is arid with scant rainfall. However, through the ingenuity of a desalinization plant, the islanders and their guests have a potable water supply. A problem solved by the intelligent application of technology and good old American know-how and can-do.

Every day that I'm on vacation I wake very early and steal downstairs by myself for an early breakfast on a terrace overlooking the beach while GM sleeps. The islanders aren't at all cynical about tourists. They're very open and talkative and ambitious. On the first day, I arrange with the cabana boy for several lounges and chairs to be set up under a thatched hut on the beach each day before I come down. I'm usually ensconced in the shade by 8 a.m. and GM joins me by 10 a.m. I'll do quite a bit of reading and enjoy the gorgeous expanse of ocean before me, as well as my fellow vacationers, who I discreetly observe from behind my sunglasses. Several times during the day, I'll swim in the pool or in the ocean. We'll leave the beach only for lunch and return to our little kingdom in the shade for the afternoon. At about 4 p.m., I'll take a long walk by myself along the water's edge. GM will read, chat with the other guests and for the most part leave me to my solitude, which she knows I cherish. I'll drink in the perfect sky and sea to my heart's content. Around 5:30, we'll go up to the room, shower and dress for dinner at a leisurely pace. Every night we'll dine at a different restaurant. On our return to the hotel, we'll play in the casino for an hour or two where I'm always impressed by GM's optimism in the face of "chance and necessity." About 10 or 11 p.m., we'll retire to our room where GM will sleep the sleep of the righteous and I'll watch a movie on cable. The next day, we'll repeat the whole itinerary again. On one afternoon, we'll go to town and I'll buy perfume, one of my vices. And that is the extent of my idyll.

Last year as I lay on my lounge looking out at the ocean, I asked myself why it had taken me so long to accomplish anything in my life. And the answer came to me that as far back as I can remember, I'd never really had a cooperative, motivated partner, someone willing to work with me toward mutual goals. That everything I'd accomplished had been despite my liaisons not because of them. I'd always had to take the long way around and by myself.

So you see, even though I would like to give Sam credit for my long-in- coming and hard earned personhood, I think if Jane hadn't died and left me with only my own life to live as her legacy, I might never have emerged at all. A painful, raw emergence made even more difficult by the many humiliations I've suffered subsequently. As if I'd let go of her hand in a crowded department store and she was gone...gone forever and because her mother had looked away for only a moment. I sometimes believe that Sam has never forgiven me for her death. I know my mother hasn't.

I felt very close to you the other evening. I think that that so solid concrete wall we both feel between us is not so much made out of our resistance, but is an owning up to our separate idiosyncrasies and the very solid and spirited integrity of our relationship. Perhaps instead of beating our heads against it, we might look over the top of it to really see each other.

Est-ce que tu me vois?

Moi-meme, sain et sauf

Jess

I'd begun by talking about my relationship with Sam and then suddenly I'd described the form and shape of a vacation, a vacation I took in solitude, accompanied only by a dear old woman who in no way intruded on that precious solitude. I hadn't vacationed with Sam for several years. Vacations had become a time for shaping personhood, a singular and independent self. Clearly I was in the midst of rewriting my life. A relationship with Sam was no longer the center of my universe. I was reminded of Michelangelo's drawing of man as the center of his own universe with all its spokes from head, hands, arms, legs.

Sam's reaction to the vicissitudes of life was to string all the bad things together and wear them like a necklace of despair--Coleridge's albatross--around his neck. He was aging rapidly under its weight. His body wasn't able to withstand the punishing effects of his depression. He drank. He raged in his sleep, cursing and fighting unknown assailants. He often felt overwhelmed by what seemed to me to be only annoying details. He ignored his diabetes, forgot his medication. He lost things. He acted helpless in front of his daughters. Daughters that he probably wished were sons. I felt bereft—I'd lost a best friend, a wonderful lover—only to have to cope with this old man who stood before me, head bowed, no longer my protector, ravaged by anger and disappointment, pain and shame. A look in the mirror told me that I was also aging. My face, something I'd always taken for granted, was changing. There was something in the eyes. I didn't always recognize parts of my body—a freckled hand or a swollen ankle. I sought to reconcile myself to this unrecognizable body, to achieve some sort of unity. Idealistic, I suppose, to struggle with the physical signs of change, to try to gracefully accept the aging process.

Wednesday, November 17, 1993

Cher ebon ami,

You are like a greedy child! You tell me that my letters are missing an ingredient — emotion. Well, they have an entire

38

rainbow of emotions when I write them! So I must conclude that you lack emotion when you read them! Perhaps, after treating so many of us, you cannot add the necessary ingredients — empathy and imagination — to these letters I write so faithfully to you. Perhaps, I tell myself, you are entirely too busy for my letters. And I do understand that. I tell myself it's probably good for me to have to acknowledge once in a while that I'm not your only patient.

It's not emotion you are seeking, my friend. What you're actually seeking are two of the keys to my letters. For when you asked me to write to you in my own handwriting, I think you were seeking what's known as "the writing beneath the erasure" of my consciousness. You want to get beyond the way in which I organize language to see what I cross out or go over with my pen, even what mistakes I make, the slips and rewrites that would reveal so much more than what I tell you. Once again, you wish to unlock, probe and explore the unknown territories of my subconscious. You're adventurous. I, on the other hand, am on a knowledge quest. That's why I read everything I can lay my hands on. So that I may apply it layer upon layer to my writing, like gesso prepares a wall for painting.

When you suggest I tape record my letters to you, however, you're suggesting something else—something vicarious that listening to the voice may expose, some loss of self-control, an abolishment of ego, perhaps. You are, I think, seeking the music of my soul. I would tell you to listen to the music of Rodrigo or Sibelius' *Finlandia*. Or "Musetta's Waltz" from *La Boheme*. I'll be seeing Boheme at the Met the Saturday I return from vacation. Actually, all of Puccini's work will tell you about my voice. Sometimes I'm the terrible voice of Turandot. And sometimes I'm the voice of Butterfly, longing for what has already been lost to her. There's something always slightly dishabille about Puccini's femmes, don't you think.

You know, I really meant it when I said that I should like to agree with you more often, but instead I find it much more valuable to define myself by what I am that you are not and what you are that I am not. You're right — to seek consensus is inevitably as boring as to constantly create social dualisms. To act as spurs to each other's thoughts and ideas is different and more positive than my acting on your advice, don't you agree? Then I don't have to always be a passive receptor. It makes for a more lively dialogue.

Nevertheless you should know by now that I don't surrender easily, especially to an idea. During our last session, even though I felt nostalgic for the person I can never be again, I was still glad you told me several things about yourself I hadn't known before. I don't underestimate the value of novelty in distracting the forlorn.

Lately, I've been thinking about big, big comfortable easy chairs. Every day on my way to work, I pass a furniture store that has an easy chair in every window. They're displayed in such inviting settings-there's an afghan and a book. A reading lamp and a book shelf. The scene just awaits an actor. When I was 12 or 13, in that lovely dormant time before I thought of boys, I used to come home after school, change into one of my grandfather's old white shirts and blue jeans and curl up in this big, overstuffed armchair to read. It was pure transport. Even now, those big chairs entice me. I suppose they are the equivalent of a car in someone else's life.

Speaking of creative substitutions, which is what I'm doing now, when I dined with my business partners and friends the other evening, we were joined by several generations of absolutely adorable dachshunds. The dogs were a delightful part of our evening, tumbling around and clambering over us, snoozing for a few minutes at our feet, offering themselves to be petted. And it occurred to me watching their owner with them that a pet is a fine consolation for what I lack — the human touch, and, in a deeper sense, the ultimate connection with another and with my own depths of passion. Sam, fearing to confront his impotency, makes fewer and fewer overtures toward me—he's forgotten all those slight, but important, physical messages that are sent well before we make love, the touch absentmindedly bestowed before we're fully conscious of our goal.

Some of the happiest moments I can recall in my life took place on Sunday mornings when the girls, all three of them, would tumble onto our bed in a jumble of arms and legs, skin and glorious tousled hair, laughing and talking and nestling between us. I, who had been so lonely as a child, was so enlarged and enhanced by their restless bodies and spirited minds. I know that in the most annealing sense, having my children was an opportunity for me to love them in the way I wished to have been loved.

I'm thinking of the ease and comfort of solitude as well as the healing properties of touch until we meet next. It is difficult to think of "purpose." But I'll try.

Jess, l'ecrivain de moi meme de plus en plus

I had discovered solace in solitude in unspoken ways that I would have scoffed at or, at the very least, taken for granted in the past when I'd held illusions about roles and relationships, life in general. Jane's birthday was coming up. GM and I would be on holiday. It was appropriate, I thought, that we two, mother and grandmother, perhaps the two who had withstood the heaviest fell stroke of her death, had, with no mention of the date, tacitly agreed to be together. The airlines were on strike and we were unsure of our flight. Nevertheless we showed up, each of us from our separate lives, at the airport that morning, not knowing what to expect, but with a shared sense of inevitability that few of our fellow passengers possessed.

Tuesday, November 23, 1993

Cher ebon ami,

Never having thought I would be here, I find myself sitting blissfully before an ideal horizon this morning! Traveling during the airline's strike was truly an existential experience. I wanted to go as much as I wanted to stay! I find that the key to handling ambiguous situations, however, lies in being able to flex that wonderful muscle — the mind. To think, my friend, to "work it

41

through" while I'm living it. That's the answer. Of course, I must be free of the negative weight of anxiety.

My island, happily, is just as I left it. We are staying in a more "comfortable" hotel this year, one that we are familiar with from other visits. It has the sort of natural decay that wind and sun and salt and weather bring, but it is home for these few days and I'm supremely content to be here. I have no ambition but to occasionally lift my eyes from my book and seek the horizon.

This morning at breakfast I watched an orange cat stalking pretty yellow birds on the terrace. On the beach, there were even more stray dogs than I remembered. A blond boy is setting up wind sails next to the hut where I'm sitting — pink and purple, yellow and orange, they wave gently in the breeze like giant butterfly wings. November clouds scud across the bluest sky in the path of fortuitous breezes. There is something real and substantial about this island situated beneath the tradewinds as it is.

This afternoon it rained — imagine my surprise! It hardly ever rains here, but it passed over in about an hour and I'm back on the beach in late afternoon light that lies silver on the horizon. GM and I went to the casino after lunch because of the weather. Playing the slots has become one of her favorite things to do — perhaps it's her age. She has so few enjoyments and asks for very little for herself. She is 77.

Soon it will be time for this mushroom in the shade to take her afternoon walk down the beach. You see, my friend, I'm very much a creature of habit, even here in my solitude. And I have been thinking about what truly isolated retreats in the Caribbean must be like, and about exclusivity and social class, human relationships and such. Sounds dreadful and unnecessarily solemn for this setting doesn't it? But it occurs to me that I do need people, if only to observe in all their constant variations (and for much more, I admit). Still, I have developed a habit of evading all that is querulous, noisy, unpleasant and frivolous about people. The forced cheerfulness of some vacationers depresses me and I seek a quieter place on the beach.

Wednesday, November 24, 1993

With only a few days here and each seeming so precious, it rains for the second day on my island paradise! And the rain heightens my sense of immediacy. I'm living in the "now" of this place. I don't live for yesterday or tomorrow. You are, in the larger sense, quite right, mon medecin bon. It is only possible to be whole, fully human in the present. In the particulars, however, you are woefully wrong. And I'm constructed of nothing but particulars. Together perhaps we can bring what it means to be "fully human" into focus.

How glad I am that I've taken this vacation without a man! Yesterday at the end of the day, while I walked the length of this lovely beach along the water's edge, it occurred to me that spending this time away from Sam and my boss, and Lenny and you, my kind interrogator, made me able to see you all as separate from me. And then, only then, was I able to view you all with true affection. You know, E.M. Forster said, "only connect." But I would say it this way: "Only cohere, only connect."

Next to me a young man in red shorts prepares a small sail boat. This section of the beach is strewn with red and blue canoes and bright red and white paddle boats today. The tiny sailboat will hold only one person — it looks inviting with its red white and blue sail that will bravely catch and hold the wind. The young man attaches a rudder. The sail tilts back and forth on its sandy mooring.

A stout middle aged European couple is bathing in the ocean as if it is a cure. With heavy tread, they move through the water, taking in the salt water, snuffling and hawking like two water buffalo, somewhere aware they are only a speck in eternal seas. It is human nature to spit in the ocean, I think.

Thursday, November 25, 1993

Yesterday turned out to be a clear beautiful day after all and we were able to have lots of beach time. Next to us in the shade, a young couple and their 18 month-old son play, eat and sleep.

The little boy is so wonderfully his own person. It makes me think about our talks about autism. But after all, I do not wish to live in such a limited world. No, rather I pray my world grows ever outward in concentric circles, but perceptibly like depth soundings in deep calm seas.

For the past several days there have been two topless bathers on the beach, blonde and lithe of limb, sun-golden. I call them the "bare breasted women." They bare their breasts only to go in the water or lie in the sun. To walk among the rest of us on the beach, they wear the tops to their suits. So it is only with sand, sea and air that they seek au naturelle congress. Like two proud venuses, they stride into the blue green Caribbean Sea together. They make me think about my own body. How heavy it has grown over the years. And how recalcitrant and slow it is to respond to my commands. I think about how ripe it was once for bearing children. A young intern once told me I was made for bearing children and I felt that certain pride that comes with being an ample and sturdy vessel.

But I can't remember a time in my childhood when I didn't feel a modesty that belied shame concerning my body. I was pale and soft when others were firm and brown. I was thin and frail and had to take tonic. I was freckled and had red hair. I yearned for the deep texture, the force and vibrancy, the coarse sensuality of dark haired people. Both my mother and my father were dark haired and so was my brother, Tom. I felt my body to be so vulnerable. Because it was a source of delicious secret pleasure, I felt the need to hide my body and then when I discovered its currency, its virginal value in the world of sexual commerce, I struggled to share it without relinquishing it, without spending it, wasting this body that had become precious for the very act of its betrayal.

Nevertheless, there is a great deal to be said for simply being able to "hold still." I discovered that my pale, vulnerable corporeal self, weak limbed and soft like the underbelly of a fish had inner strengths I could not have known about. I had a womb that held onto its sweet package though the world was set against it. Protected by the sheer physicality of inertia, no child could be shaken from its rightful place there. This body did not abort or miscarry. I felt the strength of that elliptical space within me; in utero I was strong. The first of many ironies.

Next to me, they load dozens of red oxygen tanks into sleeves on the sides of a flat-bottomed boat, preparing for the day's share of divers. A white sail moves across the horizon. Today in the States, it is Thanksgiving, but here on my island there is only wind, sand, sky and sea.

Had she lived, Janie would be 31 years old this month. Ah, my friend, the salt water calls to me and I bathe in an ocean of tears.

Friday, November 26, 1993

There is only the slightest breeze this morning and the ocean lies before me flat as glass and imperturbable. I drink in the horizon to last me for a while. At breakfast today, I wondered about you — about what it must have been like to grow up on an island. Did you also cultivate an inner and outer life? Were you protected in Jeremie from the shipfuls of tourists who came to Haiti for the warmth, for its exotic charm, for the fulsomeness of "la langue?" And where does corruption begin — from without or within? A black dog walks uncertainly toward me from the water's edge, her teats swaying flat and empty. A pair of yellow birds fly up into the rafters of my hut, then flutter away like two yellow leaves falling from a tree.

The breeze is beginning to pick up now — the islanders seem just slightly more worn, more tired of their foreign guests than I remembered. But isn't it always this way? That the weight of mutual dependency erodes enthusiasm and desire.

What is happening to me, mon psychologue? What Pandora's box have we opened with these letters of mine? The more I write to you, the more I feel I want to say. The letters have become a providential space. The text becomes jouissant in contrast to the desiccation I feel taking place in my body. And I love the contradiction.

I've finished a very good book. It's called *French Lessons* and Alice Kaplan wrote it. It is an autobiography of an American university professor of French. For her dissertation,

Kaplan studied French fascist intellectuals. Toward the end of her book, she describes her interviews with a revisionist intellectual who was a collaborator during WWII. In chill recognition, I hear the very cadences of my last master, the man I worked for during the last two and one half years. My mind does one of its usual tricks and leaps to you. For a moment, I cannot differentiate between you and this other. All that was bigoted and tyrannical of this world has overwhelmed my moral judgment and I'm "sleeping with the enemy." A collaborator. But then I go to the sea, to its vastness and its eternal properties. I swim with the sun on my face. And I remember your goodness. Jusqu'a Lundi

Moi-meme, sain et sauf

Jess

Time, ordinarily my enemy, had become my friend and repaired my thoughts. The sameness of the days, the immutable horizon, the tempered lap of waves riffling turquoise water had eased confusion.

But the session following my vacation proved to be a difficult one. I handed him the letter I'd written from the island-- my vacation as a gift--he was surprised that I hadn't been vacationing with Sam, although I'd mentioned that fact several times during sessions and in the letters. Actually, when I considered his inattention, the details of my life never held his interest, only my dialogue with him.

All during this time, I was struggling to redefine my situation at work. I'd made a conscious decision to work in non-profit because there was usually a worthy aim associated with the group. Despite the immediate and very apparent limitations of a secretarial position, the idealist in me could still feel that I was a part of something larger that had, as its end goal at least, the common good. About three years before, I'd come in from the cold, the uncertainty of working on grant money, and taken a position with a well-established trade association. Because of my experience and background, they hired me to work for their president, a thirty-year veteran. I'd reached the top of the clerical ladder; I could either settle in at this level or change careers altogether. My education seemed to demand more of me, but prudence prevailed. With little support from my family, all of whom seemed preoccupied with the uncertainties of their own situations, I felt it best to stay in what seemed to me at the time a secure backwater. That was the conscious decision.

On another, deeper, more murky level, something held me back. And it had always held me back as long as I could remember, instilling a fear, no, a terror in me of trying, of the unfamiliar and my own awkwardness, of succeeding at something that might call me away from the anonymity of the margin, away from the edge of the circle where I felt safe. Yes, oh yes, imagine succeeding at something and having the power to call attention to oneself; being seen, being recognized, people wanting things from you, expecting things from you, or, worse yet, talking about you, whispering and pointing, setting you apart. And yet I chafed at my self-restraint, felt silenced by this man, afraid to reveal my true self.

He was a complicated man, to be sure. A military man who took particular comfort in the rites and privileges, routines and customs he'd maintained for the past 30 years. A bit of a brahmin--a man who held you intentionally at a distance to be able to better relish the distinctions he made between himself and you. How he loved being him! That was why it was so strange and disconcerting to witness his retirement, to watch him relinquish his power—like watching all social certitude and center whirl into itself and disappear in the void.

I was frightened about my future. But as it turned out, I needn't have been. Secretaries, unless they believe in Viking funerals where they throw themselves on top of the funeral pyre along with the retiree's desk set and favorite coffee mug, usually survive these changing of the guard things quite well. I survived that awkward transition period when one man takes over where another left off, but I was shaken by profoundly divided loyalties, surprisingly enough. He had silenced me, held me at a distance and been coldly indifferent to me even though I sat

47

outside his office, the closest living human being to him for more than two and a half years, day in and day out. Nevertheless, I felt ambivalent about his stepping down, I worried about what he would do in retirement. Not that he had the slightest sympathy for my situation. Whether the next man picked me up or let me go was none of his concern. I would have to renegotiate my job with no help from him. I harbored no illusions about that.

He was a great teller of jokes and stories -- a real raconteur. Part of my job had been to listen intently and laugh at the appropriate moment. And I'd been a very good audience, laughing on the last day as if it were the first, never letting on that I'd heard this same story so many times, I could recite it in my sleep. What bothered me was that he never asked if he'd told me it before, a simple courtesy that one would confer on any acquaintance. But that was precisely it -- I wasn't in his world at all. I was an object. The few times I'd attempted to actually speak with him about something personal, at a certain point in the conversation he would glance at his watch.

Tuesday, November 30, 1993

Cher ebon ami,

Why don't you pay attention to me? You're distracted self disappoints me. It makes me feel superfluous. Ironic that I should suddenly menstruate after two months of nothing and that it should happen today. My daughter Jane would have been 31 years old today. The boy who was her fiancé called me today, but I was away from my desk. He remembered her birthday even after all these years. It makes me think of how extraordinary she was, all light and luminous, with a generous smile and a chaste heart. Jane. No one replaces her and nothing compensates us for having lost her. My grief today is as fresh as the day it happened.

With regard to my sex life, or should I say the demise of my sex life, I think I need to clarify the situation for you. At this point in my life, I would consider masturbation regressive. My sexuality is inextricably linked to physically connecting with another human being, specifically my husband. The fear of contamination doesn't apply here since we are monogamous, a pre-HIV couple. Admittedly as a young woman, I did fear penetration. Sexual relations with Sam, however, who was a practiced lover who had indulged his own sexual fantasies long before I came into his life, brought me in touch with my own deeply concealed passions and with my somewhat pallid fantasies. He was 33 years old and I was 26 when we met. Our sexual compatibility was never a question even under the worst conditions and most stressful times.

Now I'm faced with my partner's dysfunction. How do I deal with it. Certainly not by resuming masturbation. It would be too lonely, would remind me of my lonely childhood. Besides, I don't have enough of the narcissist in me for it. And for Sam to bring me to orgasm with a vibrator, although it is a creative substitution, is too mechanistic. It saps me of my will, puts enormous demands upon my body. No, I think that there will be sporadic returns to partial sexual potency and I will have to be satisfied with that and will eventually have to channel a good deal of sexual energy into other parts of my life. Part of growing older gracefully. I must remind myself that many people live without sexual love. Some have never known it.

But the complicity I spoke of at our last session wasn't sexual complicity. It was on its surface emotional, but on another level it was moral. For not having spoken out, even from an obviously less powerful position as the employee, I paid a heavy price with my former employer and he continued to comfortably "poison wells." Silence is indeed death. Where the bargain is silence, the soul perishes. Misperceptions flourish and the terror of in some way becoming one's persecutor begins to take hold. It is the beginning of voluntary extermination or worse, the beginning of a sick affection for the very instrument of power that silences you. I don't miss him. He had the world figured out to his satisfaction. And what I thought of as intellectual curiosity on his part was only that of someone who wants to spar and fence and play with those who are already his victims. Dear medecin, I grow fearfully tired this evening. I've come home from vacation to some hard realities. Please forgive me if I say bonne nuit, I have revenged myself on you enough for now.

Jusqu'a Lundi, I'm moi-meme, sain et sauf

Jess

    I was struggling to throw off the constrictions of my work life. I had a new boss who declared that he would have to "deprogram" me after my stint in the military. The first thing he did was put up pictures of his wife and kids in his office. But, as always, I was trying to make sense out of the past, to figure out exactly what the last few years had meant in my life.

Tuesday, December 7, 1993

Cher ebon ami,

    How good it is to sleep on our last session! A deep, dreamless sleep, a sleep that repairs and clarifies. A sleep so peaceful that I awake without regret.
    So many threads unraveled last evening as we talked. It is as if we are playing out a ball of string in this therapy. It is in this almost involuntary motion of playing out line, letting out the skeins of my life that I find the most truth. And e.e. cummings, one of my favorite poets wrote:

> what a wonderful thing
> is the end of a string
> (murmurs little you-i
> as the hill becomes nil)
> and will somebody tell
> me why people let go

    I wonder if you understand my motives for what may seem to you a preoccupation with my own physical health. Actually, my concern only emerged in the last few years. It has to do with accepting responsibility for my body, staying alert to what it tells me, despite what others may tell me, and trying to keep it healthy in a positive, reaffirming way. We Scorpios have a dark side, a tendency toward exploring the less healthy side of our natures. And you have given it a name! Involutional melancholia! Well, responsibly taking care of my physical self is part of the cure for that. It helps to blow away the scary, slightly morbid tales of sickness and disease, overblown descriptions and angry new red scars that were part of my mother's repertoire — the near escapes, the hospital heroics with never an insight or a rational explanation. It is a wonder I know what "normal" means in terms of human bodies.

It is no accident, you know, that I spoke of both Sam and my mother in our last session. Both have been powerful figures in my life, both are objects of love, whose hysteria I dutifully absorbed and then discreetly dealt with at great cost. What astonished me was finally being able to admit that Sam was not the most central figure in my life. That I was. Almost at the same time that I spoke those words, I felt the weight of their meaning. Implicit to that realization is a shift in how I view myself. How casual I sound, but how great a weight lifts from me as I write this.

I think you underestimate the value of an education. For years I was afraid to grow beyond the perimeter of my mother's life. Part of moving beyond her is being able to appraise her life, yes, even judge her life, for what I can learn from it. Years ago I learned that she would provide no role model for me. During a stressful period in my life, I asked myself, "what would my mother do?" The answer was she'd run away, she'd drink herself into oblivion, she'd indulge in maudlin bouts of self-pity. None of these were viable or acceptable solutions for me. Better to ask, "what wouldn't my mother do?"

I received your holiday card today and thank you for sending it to me. It was strange to see your handwriting. There was something reassuring about receiving it today, after last evening's terrible random act of violence on the LIRR. My boss was very concerned when I came in this morning and, of course,

I was moved by his concern. His wife even called to see if I was all right.

Today he spoke to me about attending the Annual Meeting in Florida in the future. He'd said he'd like to have me there because of the way I deal with people. His complete faith in me acts like a tonic. Somehow he has worked past the episode in May. The more he includes me, of course, the more willing I am to give him the benefit of years of expertise. I hadn't realized what a profound effect all the distancing and exclusion his predecessor practiced had on me as well as on my work.

Kindly interrogator, ask me that question again. Remember the question you asked when I told you about looking in the mirror and being able to rely on who I would find there. You asked if I was experiencing life or .....? I have blocked it out. Yet, somehow I feel the answer would be both. I live life on more than one level, as you well know. It's just that I've gotten a lot of mileage out of that lady in the mirror. That is my "book" value. Ironic that I wish my book value was in real books. Only by living in the rich intricacies of the "life of the mind" can I forget about the lady in the mirror, only by reading and writing am I able to stave off age and death. I live among words, in fields of language and symbols. It's a charming myth, isn't it?

With winter deepening, I feel the life of spring. Perhaps that's why I quoted from e.e. cummings—for me he's the quintessential poet of springtime. Let me end this letter with the closing paragraph from his introduction to *New Poems:*

> Miracles are to come. With you I leave a remembrance of miracles; they are by somebody who can love and who shall be continually reborn, a human being;... nothing proving or sick or partial. Nothing false, nothing difficult or easy, small or colossal. Nothing ordinary or extraordinary, nothing emptied or filled, real or unreal; nothing feeble and known or clumsy and guessed. Everywhere tints childrening, innocent spontaneous, true. Nowhere possibly what flesh and impossibly such a garden, but actually flowers which breasts are among the very mouths of light.

Nothing believed or doubted; brain over heart, surface: nowhere hating or to fear; shadow, mind without soul. Only how measureless cool flames of making; only each other building always distinct selves of mutual entirely opening; only alive. Never the murdered finalities of wherewhen and yesno, impotent nongames of wrongright and rightwrong; never to gain or pause, never the soft adventure of undoom, greedy anguishes and cringing ecstasies of inexistence; never to rest and never to have: only to grow. Always the beautiful answer who asks a more beautiful question.

Perhaps I will read it to you next time I see you. It really needs to be read aloud. Jusqu'a Lundi, I remain

Moi-meme, sain et sauf

Jess

I'd stumbled on an old favorite, e.e. cummings, and he'd grasped immediately the elliptical beauty of the poetry. I'd always thought of cummings as the poet laureate of springtime. I was surprised at Bernard's enthusiasm for cummings, really remarkable that he should take to this poetry, considering English was not his first language--Creole was, but he lived in French.
The year was drawing to a close and I was in high spirits, always the prelude to a descent into depression. And it would come—come stalking me in the deepest part of the winter—after the holidays. In the meantime, I was surprised and a little bemused by his utter lack of festivity. I found him devoid of all of those cultural markers that even the least assimilated of our population held sacred. I asked about his plans for the holidays. He had none, but his wife was urging him to participate, attend church services, trim a tree, put up lights. He never did decorate the outside of the house, although he told me he intended to. His workload at the hospital always increased around this time of

year. This year, he told me, was particularly bad, with many repeaters, people who had not been in the hospital for years, returning to the ward.

Friday evening, December 24, 1993

Cher ebon ami,

Joyeux noel, mon jeune sauvage! I have just finished baking Christmas cookies and I'm preparing to drive into the city this evening for a special midnight concert at Carnegie Hall. We've attended this concert every Christmas Eve for the last 20 years. Tonight's program will be from Bach and Vivaldi. Sam and I will meet two other couples in Chinatown for dinner and then we'll all go to the concert together. It's a very pleasant tradition that has evolved over the years. But of course, you wouldn't approve of evolution. It requires that one draw upon one's past to determine one's future acts!

I have the distinct sensation of being able to gather the various strands of my life into my own hands these days. There's a sense of completion and of some anticipation. Very much like those first moments before one opens a book. There's even a certain curiosity about the future. Now that's something I never thought I would regain. The heart, strange as it may seem, does heal. One's expectations are muted by other, deeper considerations, the tendency to want to simply reach out and connect with everything human. Despite your protestations that we cannot know death nor really experience life, it is very good to be alive, to be feeling among others who are also feeling, to be loyal to someone or something as the evening deepens and the icy world sparkles in hard diamond silence. If there's one thing I've learned, my bon medecin, it is that Nature is uncaring, indifferent, and it is only through the irrepressible, resistant, enduring, indefatigable and infinitely expansive human spirit that I exist.

This week I received a shipment of books I'd ordered from Yale University Press. What a treat it is to unpack each pristine volume only waiting for me to turn back its pages, to unlock whatever it has to give.

And look what I found as I turned a page to find a publication date...some words from Albert Camus, who I've also been reading lately.

> Art, in a sense, is a revolt against everything fleeting and unfinished in the world. Consequently, its only aim is to give another form to reality that it is nevertheless forced to preserve as the source of its emotion. In this regard we are all realistic, and no one is.

You and I don't really disagree—it is a matter of where we place our emphasis. For you, the emphasis must be on the present, for me the present is only possible because of the past and in light of the future.

I'll be spending Christmas day with the babies—my godchildren. On Sunday, I'll rest and regroup because I'm off from work on Monday, but Monday evening I'm giving a 50th birthday party for one of my oldest and dearest friends. So I'm busy, but it's a good time of high sociability. As I grow older, I become increasingly more convinced that everything has its time and the trick is to know when to advance and when to withdraw. All of this is part of becoming self-sustaining, self-nurturing and at the same time broadening my world, establishing myself as part of small communities. It occurs to me that I've placed far too much importance on forming perfect personal relationships, on holding my family to some unreachable ideal.

Well, my brave adversary, I'll write to you again before the year is out. I wish you and your family all the joys and delights of the holiday season.

Moi-meme, sain et sauf

Jess

Wednesday evening, December 29, 1993

Cher ebon ami,

How I've missed you this past week! I marvel, as the year draws to its end, at all we've shared in that providential space beneath your house (with the entire house on our backs, as you put it!) a subterranean world rich with ideas, memories, dreams, hopes, fears and always the quickening of imagination, always the soothing balm of mercy. You've been generous and brave, mon medecin bon. You've quenched my thirsty curiosity and fed my appetite for recognition. You've met my anger and dried my tears. I wonder if you realize how ingenuously revealing, how truly candid you've been about yourself, particularly in the last few months. I can say now that I know you, know you as you are, know the differences between us, know the samenesses. No longer are you merely a distant authority figure, working some mysterious alchemy over my shattered thoughts. I think we've broken through the ordinary barriers to find the extraordinary in this therapeutic process—tolerance, trust and friendship. But enough. I don't want to pay you too much tribute. I have enough indebtedness in my life. Suffice to say you're funny and lighthearted, absentminded and touchingly naive, a true believer, and I find I can make neither a god nor a slave of you (but that is not to say I won't try to do so in the future!).

Strangely enough, as the New Year approaches, my main concern is to be able to write. Since the advent of these letters to you (valuable to me because of their intimate nature and for a freeing up of my most innermost thoughts) I'm at a loss to produce much else. Perhaps I'm too content with what is. Too actively involved to be able to stand apart, to prowl the margin as I'm used to doing. Or it may simply be that since I'm no longer in school, I suffer no deadlines, no exacting taskmaster.

I think I should set myself to simply explicate one of the books I'm reading. Perhaps you will be my taskmaster and I will send the finished product to you. (Utterly futile since I can barely hold your attention with my letters and they are completely immediate!)

My daughter, Mimi, leaves for school in several weeks. It's paradoxical that I'm concerned about writing, when I know it will be very different here without her at home. But that's only one of the many paradoxes I live with these days. For example, why is Sam so gentle and kind now that he's no longer sexually virile. I experience a level of comfort at home that I haven't felt for a long while. I'm much freer to express myself than I've been allowed in the past. We've just spent four full days at home together. I've been able to deal with his occasional anxious moments much more directly and easily than in the past. There's less avoidance on my part, less sheltering of feeling and consequently, less withdrawal on his part. Can I trust these changes? And to what do I owe this amnesty? Is it that he no longer feels he must dominate and control me as if I was some irrational part of him that must be held in check? Has he surrendered his misperceptions about masculinity to the all forgivingness of simple companionship? Or have we both simply risen once again from a deathlike inertia that grabs at our heels and insinuates itself within our hearts?

I watched a wonderful movie last evening called *The Natural*. The story was written by Bernard Malamud and its about two people who are overcome by fate or destiny. At one point, Glenn Close said these lines: "I believe we have two lives. The life we learn with and the life we live with after." Perhaps Sam and I are in our second life. Our denouement. In any event, I can only surmise on the eve of the New Year.

Several weeks ago, I ran into one of the patients from Mercy in a neighborhood restaurant. She was having her lunch. I knew because she had that heavily medicated look that she wouldn't remember me. But I went over and said hello to her anyway. She had been much livelier, much more resilient and spirited when we were in the hospital together. She was loaded with medication and labored at the simple function of feeding herself and navigating her way out of the restaurant. Still she *was* functioning, a tribute to her will and to the mental health program that she attended.   She'd said she attended the day program at Mercy.

I couldn't help comparing myself to her. My world was so much wider, my life so much more rich with nuances and insights, my horizon held so much more promise, my eyes were so much more sighted, I had music and books, humor and pathos, love and work. Truly, Michel Bernard, there must be a God, and there but for the grace of God go I. And I'm very glad that you accepted me as a patient, all raw and wounded, confused and mortified as I was on that day that you studied me across the day room with such bemusement when Dr. Ciaclos waved me over. Happy New Year, a healthy, happy and prosperous year to you and your wife and son. I want for you, my friend, only what you want for yourself.

Jusqu'a Lundi, je suis moi-meme, sain et sauf

Jess

Just after the holidays, everyone at work pushed full speed ahead toward the Annual Meeting.   Tension was high to outperform our effort of the previous year. I was keenly aware of being a part of a highly visible, real life group.   But somewhere in the back of my mind, I was aware of that other, invisible group, the people on the psych unit.

Wednesday evening, January 5, 1994

Cher ebon ami,

This is a very busy time for me at work. Our annual meeting and industry convention take place the last week of January and I'm responsible for a great deal of convention material as well as the docket for the Board of Directors' meeting there. So it's difficult to pick up our conversation where we left it at the end of our last session, but I'll try since it seems to me we were getting

58

into unexplored territory and that makes for good therapy, don't you agree?

Let me see, if I'm correct, I think we were talking about the kind of conspiratorial therapy that goes on among mental patients most of the time unbeknownst to their caretakers. Yes, there's an invisible network among us, particularly in "containment." There are the offhand remarks we make to each other as we stand obediently in line for medication. One may pour a paper cup of water for another as if it's holy water, ancient and from some savage source. It may be as simple a gesture as suddenly choosing to sit with someone at the same table for a meal, or sharing some verboten object like a hairdryer, or braiding a woman's hair for her. It may be the code-like banter between teams playing an outré game of shuffleboard under the watchful scrutiny of the caretakers. It's an underground of interaction and resistance played out in a glance, a word, and if you listen for it, you'll hear the patients, each from their own fine insanity, like birds in the bare boughs of trees in winter, sing to each other of their particular afflictions. Most caretakers can't hear it, because they're too busy singing their own songs to us, and because they're usually only aware of the power and responsibility of surveillance. But it exists and where it does, it brings hope and is a reminder of the remarkable resilience people have and that their need to reach out beyond the boundaries of psychic pain in order to touch one another is strong. Because you're right about psychic pain, my friend, and how unbearable it becomes. And the heroic struggle to reclaim one's sanity often can't be accomplished without reclaiming one's anger, throwing off whatever oppresses the spirit, real and imagined. I only know that in this upward spiral from depression, one must pass through a spectrum of emotions, of feelings, in order to "only live." Yet you would say we ask to be contained.

From *Woman on the Edge of Time*, a novel by Marge Piercy, here is a description of the function of a mental hospital in a feminist utopia:

Our madhouses are places where people retreat when they want to go down into themselves—to collapse, carry on, see visions, hear voices of prophecy, bang on walls, relive infancy—getting in touch with the buried self and the inner mind. We all lose parts of ourselves. We all make choices that go bad....How can another person decide that it is time for me to disintegrate, to reintegrate myself?

I'm struck by your being drawn toward what you fear most. It's the very antithesis of the common philosophy — to avoid pain and seek the pleasurable. Still, this avoidance of the unpleasant or painful elements of life often deters me from achieving the goals that my inner self desires. For instance, I haven't submitted any material for publication this last year for fear of rejection. Over all my actions and non-actions hovers an all-pervading awareness of the purely arbitrary and accidental nature of life. The sort of thing you enjoy and I view with dread and foreboding. We are, indeed, very different from each other, you and I.

Nevertheless, I'm eager to see you again, and I remain, I assure you, jusqu'a Lundi,

Moi-meme, sain et sauf

Jess

We were to have sixteen snow storms that winter. We'd already been hit hard by bitter cold temperatures and ice storms. I remember for the first time being totally unsure of my footing as I walked from the train to my office. One of the few reassurances I had was the knowledge that he was showing up for his job at the hospital. I imagined all sorts of protection for myself. Phalanxes of Haitian men sitting unobtrusively on my train, rising to depart when I did, walking in front of me and behind me as I trudged the narrow walkways where some good samaritan had shoveled a path, as I crossed the sheet ice streets of Manhattan, my feet leaden in heavy rubber boots, afraid, so afraid of falling. Physical hazards presented themselves to me with every footfall. I was a prisoner to my own fears. I felt isolated and alone. I felt the presence of some unknown danger. Only the thought of him also braving the weather kept me coming to work. It was a struggle and I was starting to show signs of breaking.

On one of the darkest days of that horrible winter, he confessed to me that he feared snakes; that the sight of a snake made him coil in fear, but at the same time he was drawn to it. He said we're inexorably drawn to what we fear the most. Was this true for me? Did I fear madness, but also feel drawn to its depths? At work, the pressure was on. Those of us who didn't go down to the convention in Florida to work were left to fend for ourselves. The office had the quiet deserted look of a ghost ship. Survival seemed to lie in just continuing to write the letters and in reading, voracious reading.

Tuesday evening, January 12, 1994

Cher ebon ami,

A word you used at our last session has been buzzing around in my head and now I find that it's in none of my dictionaries (of which I have many!). I wonder if it's not of French derivation. The word is "subjure." I immediately understood it when you used it in context. But then afterwards, I felt that I wanted to understand better what it meant to be "subjured."

Why do I want so keenly for you to know me? I tell myself that perhaps it's impossible to ever really know another person. Yet, if I'm to have any importance at all in the scheme of things, it will be, I think, through expressivity — in not only finding my own voice, but in using that voice to express that which is "subjured."

At times I think it must be easy to be you, self assured and grounded. You know what you know. You don't doubt what you know. You don't question your capabilities. Mountains are only there to climb, death remains an enigma, all of life corresponds if only one can find the fit, for every question there is a rational answer and only the immediate present counts for anything. When the sun shines so directly overhead, one casts no shadow. Perhaps that's what I seek. To be your shadow. It would be a strange kind of modeling. You would see me before you and sometimes over your shoulder. The outline of the shadow would be your reflection, but the indefinable and silent depths of its darkness, its content, would be my province. And to see your shadow might make you pause and reflect. Perhaps you might reflect upon what is immutable and given, dictated by external realities beyond reasonable comprehension. Realities which necessitate not just the reconstruction of a life, but its very reinvention, not just adaptiveness, but rebirth and the rekindling of emotion.

Yet, I recall your telling me how heavy a burden psychology/philosophy was to you at times. Do I wish to add to your burden by insisting that you know me. Where is the good in my deliberately limning our differences? What do I expect from you? You have demonstrated your tolerance many times over. I think I want to leave some sort of mark on you. A kind of continuous, yet subtle, sign of my own immortality, much like water makes on rock or wind on a stand of trees after a long time. As if to say, "I passed this way and left this mark as a sign of my endurance and his good durability."

I'm reading Dr. Robert Jay Lifton's most recent book on the protean self. I had the privilege of studying with him in a seminar last year. Lifton maintains that there are psychobiological differences between men and women. Here is some of what he has to say:

> Although Proteus is male, there is virtually no manifestation of the protean self that either sex cannot express. Any differences are mainly in nuance. Men are given more opportunity by society, especially in connection with occupation, to experiment with forms and combinations. Women, on the other hand, perform (at least in American society) a special form of protean juggling in combining commitments to home, childbirth,

and nurturing, with occupational and intellectual pursuits. At the same time, women in our study were more focused on grounding, more concerned with sustaining intimate relationships and relationships in general. That overall emphasis upon connection can discourage protean exploration in some women. But in others it contributes to that exploration either by providing elements of structure that free one for bold protean forays or by suggesting an ideal model (of, say, significant work or an authentic relationship) for what one constantly seeks... *The Protean Self: Human Resilience in an Age of Fragmentation*, p.9

What do you think? I'm not sure about psychobiological differences, but I never had the intellectual resources to argue that with him (he invited me to do so in a critique he gave on one of my papers).

It's true, as you mentioned at the end of our last session, that I'm worried about a relapse. More about that when we meet next Monday. Suffice to say, I'm thinking about borrowed power or the bad habit of vicarious experience and about my own need for acknowledgement and recognition. About answered and unanswered prayers.

Jusqu'a Lundi, I continue to be

Moi-meme, sain et sauf

Jess

Wednesday evening, January 19, 1994

Cher ebon ami,

You suggested last session that I lack structure in my life. You also reopened the subject of my diagnosis. I'm very heartened and in some indefinable way, relieved, by your pronouncement that my illness is not a bi-polar one. It's good to know what I'm not from what I am. It helps to further define me.   Actually, I think that the very first diagnosis made was probably the most descriptive of my illness—anxiety depression. I would diagnose myself along these lines. There is, first of all, implicit in this diagnosis the recognition of dread as an appropriate reaction to perceived experience.   Also its complementarity to anger evoked by feelings of powerlessness. Depression, it has been said, is repressed anger.   I think if I didn't have such an active imagination I wouldn't feel dread. And all avenues of escape, ego diffusion, empathy, daydreaming, reading, would be less accessible to me. I suppose you would have me make something positive out of all of this, but I view it as something immoderate and unbalanced.   I only know that there's a deep and rebellious streak in my nature that's very sensitive to the injustices perpetrated by the "haves" upon the "have nots." And that I can't live my life without some sense of agency, without some intimation of authenticity, without some mark of my immortality.

I'm reading a truly fascinating book and despite your editorial comments on my "free associating" I'd like to tell you a little about it. It's called *Holocaust Testimonies: The Ruins of Memory* and it's written by Lawrence Langer. It deals with the unique properties of oral testimony and the psychological phenomenon of *dedoublement*. During my first year of graduate studies, I wrote about testimony, particularly the testimony of women and children as part of a cultural matrilineage, for a final exam in a women studies course. My paper was called Cultural Matrilineage: Pieces of the Puzzle and in it I talked about "subjective authenticity."

> Ironically, the testimony of women and children has been systematically ignored in patriarchal society. The patriarchy usually demands that a witness be impartial and innocent of any underlying agenda, contrary to the idea of subjective authenticity, and that the testimony given reflect these qualities.

Oddly enough, much of what the former victims of the Holocaust describe or, I should say, struggle to describe, is quite familiar to me, especially since the death of my daughter. The book deals with memory in categories: deep memory: the buried self, anguished memory: the divided self, humiliated memory: the besieged self, tainted memory: the impromptu self, and unheroic memory: the diminished self. The aim of the book is

> to attempt to make the events speak through the individual and in his language, to rescue the suffering from huge numbers, from dreadful anonymity, and to restore the person's given and family name, to give the tortured person back his human form, which was snatched away from him.

Further, the author writes, "When human beings ceased to be emissaries or legatees of love and became instead agents or victims of power on such a massive scale, we may have witnessed a shift in civilization's priorities with whose psychological bequest we continue to struggle." Ah, my friend, there is so much I would like you to know from this book, so much I should like to "copy onto your mind" as if I could copy it from one computer to another. But why? I ask myself why I want you to read what I read, know what I know. Perhaps it's because I wish to conjoin what I know in my deep memory, where there is no place to hide and no longer any illusions, with the common memory, memory of normalcy and continuity, form and coherence.

I'm feeling overwhelmingly ashamed of myself for having lost self-control at work. I will speak with you on Monday. In the meantime, I remain,

Moi-meme, sain et sauf

Jess

Tuesday evening, January 25, 1994

Cher ebon ami,

I think we touched on several important themes in our last session — important for both of us. I believe that what I was trying to describe to you were feelings of being not helpless or powerless, but **defenseless.** It's a subtle, but important distinction, since when we talk about defenses, or even the construction of defenses, we're already a step beyond the formation of ego and headed toward the appropriate mechanisms for protecting one's ego. We're out of the woods, so to speak. Instead of feeling helpless or powerless, I'm feeling particularly vulnerable. But feelings of vulnerability imply that I have something to protect — an ego. Small, fragile, decentered, perhaps, but an ego nevertheless! Cette une triomphe!

It's interesting that I experience these feelings of vulnerability most keenly in relation to my daughter Mimi, both in my relationship with her and when I'm called upon to stand up for her, to defend her. Or when I must stand back and just watch her make her way on her own. What's at the bottom of my anguished feelings as spectator?

When we moved into the house, Mimi was just four years old. In fact, when we first looked at the house, even before we bought it, I remember imagining Mimi sitting in the breakfast nook eating cereal and looking out the window at the backyard. I just knew that it was the house for us, when I pictured her sitting there. That same year, Sam and I were driving somewhere in Oceanside and Mimi was sitting between us on the front seat of the car when we pulled up to a stoplight and a man in the car next to us began making anti-Semitic remarks to Sam. The incident turned my stomach and forever left a mark for me on our move to the Island. That was the same year Sam's mother died, the one person who loved Mimi unqualifiedly.

Two years later, in February, Sam's brother's 19 year-old daughter, deeply depressed, slashed herself repeatedly, took drugs and alcohol and crept out a window to her death 22 stories below. Mimi, who was six at the time, was standing next to me when I got the phone call. At the end of that year, she went in for an operation to repair a kidney problem. That was in 1977. In 1981, I was hospitalized at Mercy. Mimi's pediatricians had put her on a "diet" and I was trying to adhere to it, preparing special foods for her, etc. One of her doctors had intimated that the excess weight was the cause of her kidney problems. It was only several years later, when I looked at pictures of Mimi taken before her operation, that I realized she'd put on the weight *after* the operation. She'd been a normal weight before. Being a nurturing mother to Mimi became increasingly difficult. On some level, I was afraid of her, of her strength, and I ceded a great deal of parental authority to her. On another level, I felt enormous guilt for having brought on her physical difficulties. Always beneath the surface was the hint of tainted blood or bad genes. When I try to pin it down, it has to do with what I feel is an illicit sexuality, my own feelings of sexual transgression.

About a year later, my stepbrother, 40 years old, put a gun to his head and shot himself to death. My stepfather was never the same. He developed bleeding ulcers and then bladder cancer. In September of 1985, I received news of Jane's death. Mimi was next to me when I got the phone call. We were alone in the house at the time. I started to walk out the front door — not knowing where I was going, just that I needed to flee the horror of what I'd just heard. Mimi was at my side. Luckily, a good friend was just pulling into our driveway. She'd come to show me a new dress she'd bought. Very gently she steered us both back into the house. I remember drinking a shot of whiskey neat, feeling the heat of it in my throat.

A year later, my father died. The cancer had spread through his body and to his brain. A year after he died, when my mother abandoned us to return to Chicago, it was Mimi she told of her plans.

My point in relating all of this to you is that in her relatively short life, Mimi has experienced a great many obstacles, disruptions, and yes, losses. Her history is indelibly tied to mine and to the time of most upheaval for the entire family. She's grown up in the period of least illusion for all of us. She's become my Achilles heel, the living history of the most difficult years of my life. Even as I write this, I feel selfish.

Yes, my perception shaper, this is about "choiceless choices." But also, as you so gently suggested (and I do appreciate your gentleness), it's about the "management of choices" and about not allowing one's options to narrow. In my case, it must also be about not allowing the options to grow increasingly narrow for my children. My real, physical, flesh and blood, palpably felt, children. Jane, I must remind myself, no longer needs me.

You asked me what my defenses are. I think I must answer in a most incomplete and open way: to stay as close to the top layer of my skin as possible without losing it, without losing my outline, without losing my shadow, without losing my mind, without losing my humanity. I seek a certain permeability, you see. In any event, it is a wonderful question. Reminds me of e.e. cummings' "Always the beautiful answer who asks a more beautiful question."

This writing repairs my soul. Jusqu'a Lundi, mon medecin bon, I am

Moi-meme, sain et sauf

Jess

I was making progress — real progress. Yet I always felt as if I was standing on a precipice. And then, for some reason — probably to resolve some hidden conflict, a contradiction in my nature so deep and destructive that it couldn't find a voice but was only a shadow, an unspoken instinct that ran parallel to my ascent -- I decided to end the letters.

February 7, 1994

Dear gentle friend,

I've been thinking about the difference between being sexually alive and being sexually explicit. Ah, I'm born. A girl child in the Promised Land of Chicago 1941. A redheaded monster, a firebrand. No, the circumstances of my birth are really quite ordinary. Except that it was no ordinary time. There was war in the air. Everywhere the smell of tinder and ashes. And over everything, the mewing squall of the secondborn, their hands outstretched supplicating, supplicating. Only I didn't know anything of it. Born ingenuously enough at Augustana Hospital in the aftermath of the last age of innocence, when nurses printed babies feet on birth certificates.

When I was four or five years old, I wore my brother's hand-me-down clothes. I can still remember sitting on the curb in a pair of his overalls and a striped tee shirt, eating watermelon with a bunch of other kids; we were spitting the seeds far out into the street and were waiting for something to happen. That something was the emergence of the bride and groom from the church across the street. And when they stepped into the clear spring sunshine, pausing for one moment, caught off guard by the force of the white light after the dim interior of the church, my brother jumped up off the curb and, always the leader of our little band, enjoined us to yell "suckerrr" at them. And so we did. I yelled it loud and long, even though I had no idea what I was yelling or even why I was yelling it at that imperturbably happy couple just stepping into a limousine to be whisked away—to what fate I couldn't imagine.

That was probably the last time in my life that I was completely innocent, that I said something without thinking about what I was saying, that I followed anyone, including my brother with absolute trust and obedience. I remember with what relish I called out the word -- "suckerrrr" -- was it meant to cheer them on or was it said with a sneer of derision?

Later I would find that it meant that a woman was a sort of natural trap and a man got *suckered* into marrying her -- he was seduced by her feminine wiles and lost his good sense just long enough for her to haul him up to the altar where his future was signed, sealed and delivered into domesticity. Caught in a con -- that's why we yelled "sucker"-- because she'd tricked him into marrying her, she with the big white dress and billowing veil, veiled so that he couldn't see her. Couldn't see what the future

69

held, all the days of waking up with her face on the pillow next to him, all the face to face conversations that would take place in their lifetime, all the cheerful hellos and tearful goodbyes finally written on her face, etched as if they were engraved by some master artisan at the corners of her eyes, grooved smiles on the apples of her cheeks, spidery lines at the lip's expression. And when you turned your back on her was she still there? Or did she go away to some deep uncharted territory, ghastly and deep. She could swallow you up, sucker.

Or was I really yelling, in my worn old corduroys and faded tee shirt, "succor" —given the word as my birthright – to give comfort and aid, rest and nurture to the uneasy, an uneasy combination at best, yes, that's what marriage is – everyone getting into the narrow wedding bed with you, resting on the thin pallet of new emotions, so thin you can feel the rocky roadbed beneath your shoulder blade, cutting into you, for aren't you always on your back, sister? And from there it's a long climb to the heights, but you give him a good ride, sister. Pump! Pump with your legs-- you know how--make that swing go up, up into the air, cool blue ether.

In those days there were empty or vacant lots for us to play in. My shoes were always scuffed from running down the alleyway, paved with cinders then, no asphalt. I would be running to keep up with my brother and his friends, running fast and then I'd have to drop to one knee, pull up my stockings, unbuckle my shoe to rid myself of those cinders. Nowhere more alone than that, kneeling in the hot sun in the alley, as if a stopwatch had suddenly stopped ticking. There were "victory" gardens all along the alley behind the apartments. I remember one afternoon I wandered into one and pulled up a carrot and ate it straight from the ground. It was warm from the sun and sweet and crunchy.

In the vacant lot, we'd dug a deep hole and lined it with pieces of linoleum. At the bottom were bricks we'd fashioned into a pit for roasting wieners and marshmallows on sticks. We tossed potatoes in and let them roast and blacken and ate them with our hands. My hair was long and hadn't yet been cut. My mother would warn me away from the bonfires. "Your hair will catch on fire," she'd say.

It was 1946 and all the kids wanted to do was play "war." I remember sitting in a branch of a tree in the sand lot waiting for the "wounded," watching the boys battle it out with broomsticks and pretend artillery. Once in a while they'd all stop to look at the real fighter planes that flew over and my brother would identify them. There goes a B-25, he'd say, or a "spitfire."

On summer nights, the smell of the slaughterhouse, heavy and hot-blooded, would spread west slowly from the stockyards on just a puff of a breeze from the lake. After dark, I'd play outside our tavern in the pool of light the neon sign in the window made on the sidewalk, all around me and down the block was darkness, except for a hazy bluish moon set high in the summer sky. Nothing else smelled like that bloody, meaty smell, filling our nostrils and stirring us from whatever we were doing. The scent of entrails, of brains and hooves and hearts, made our heads turn ever so slightly and we stirred uneasily, shifting our bodies, settling for a moment to sniff the air, and then shaking it off, the music from the juke box drifting out from the screened door of the tavern and trails of blue cigar smoke curling silkily through the screen. I hated to come in, but finally she'd remember me.

We used the stone wash tubs in the basement of the building for a bathtub and most evenings, I fell asleep on their bed behind the partition that hid our living space from the barroom. Then, after they closed, usually around three in the morning, they'd set out two army cots and we'd sleep, my brother and I, in the front among the smoky sawdust swept remains of the evening until morning came pouring through the front door of the tavern. But sometimes I'd be half dressed before I woke up — she'd be putting my socks and shoes on in the middle of the night. Then they'd carry us out to the car and we'd go to an all night joint for chicken in the basket, just the four of us. We were four.

From such beginnings is made the stuff of my life. But larger, more immediate questions are raised as I write these letters to you. Your forced cheerfulness these past few sessions, for instance. Why do you deny my experience of you? Why do

71

I only feel my triumphs as if I'm under water? Why do I remain so marginalized? I want to break out of this tomb in which I live, but these past weeks seem so reminiscent of other times in my life. The question continues to be one of "desensitization." How much should I care?   I believe in a multi-layered personality and that we have found our mutual voice by allowing for many levels of consciousness. The letters no longer actually need your address as much as they need your good heart and your precision. Let's talk about it when next we meet. Jusqua Lundi, I remain

Moi-meme, sain et sauf

Jess

Part Two

I'd had a setback -- nothing serious enough to be hospitalized for, but enough of a dip to put me out of commission for a few days at home -- I wasn't sleeping well and my concentration was shaky. February had never been a good month for me. There was so much that seemed unresolved in the early spring.

Mimi had gone off to live on campus. I was unprepared for the anxieties this separation would kick over or the gaping chasm she would leave between Sam and me after her departure. What really broke my heart was how she'd packed herself up -- everything she would ever need or want was neatly and carefully assembled on the third floor waiting to be transported to her room in the dorm at school. The most solicitous mother could not have sent her daughter away more lovingly than Mimi was sending herself. I'd done nothing. I should have known then that she was in trouble. How could I have missed the signs?

At home, I was confronted with the same old problems. Sam had no work. The house was cold and dark most evenings when I came home from work. His inertia was like a cap on whatever life I felt or hoped for. I called Dr. Bernard and asked if I could bring Sam in with me to our next session. It seemed to me that Sam was hovering, watching me for any signs of a break. Bernard agreed so readily and easily, I was instantly reassured. Maybe I could beat this thing after all.

I was so pleased with the sort of instant understanding that Bernard and I had with each other that I suppose I never fully understood how Sam must have felt during that session. Excluded where he never had been excluded before. I was able to clearly and concisely describe my symptoms to Bernard and he in turn responded quickly and decisively. I would start on medication immediately, return to work in a few days. Sam had trouble understanding Bernard because of his pronounced accent (I found a comforting rhythm in it, but it did require a practiced listener). But then Sam wasn't there to listen. That was his first mistake. He thought he would be able to unburden himself. He thought he could ride in on my wave, but this doctor was unmistakably treating me and only me. He seemed politely indifferent to Sam's litany of complaints. And when he asked Sam to wait in the outside office so that we might have some private time in the session, he turned to me right after Sam closed the office door behind him and offered to put me in the hospital. He said he didn't see how I could get well at home under these circumstances. I thanked him for the offer, I knew it was only benevolent, but I couldn't. I felt I would jeopardize my work situation.

Actually, it's difficult to describe what happened at that session, but it was a long in coming victory for me. I was handling my own illness, managing it without intervention. Ordinarily in the past Sam would have established a separate relationship with the doctor and they would've made all the decisions. From a certain point on I would have been deemed not only powerless to help myself, but also not responsible for what was happening to me. Now I was beginning to own up to my illness. And the alliance that Michel Bernard and I had formed these many months was too strong to be disallowed.

Tuesday, February 15, 1994

Cher ebon ami,

I want to thank you for protecting my space, so to speak, in our last session. You referred to the "therapeutic alliance," something that has come to mean a great deal to me and which I believe we have built together in these last several months. It is inviolable.

It's a rocky road I travel these days and all I can do to maintain my balance. God, I was surefooted years ago! But now so much seems to depend upon my judgment. I'd like to devote some time to scholarly pursuits and since you and I both know that human beings operate on more than one level and that exponential change is the name of the game for our time, I'd also like to do other things. Play. I haven't allowed myself to play for a very long time.

I've climbed up to my attic this morning with a large thermos of coffee and don't intend to "stand down" or "go below" for a while. I have everything I need here. I only wish that I could be free of the medication so that my concentration and focus could be as acute as before. But I must be patient with myself. These things have a way of defining themselves without any help from me.

I've been reading some of Emily Dickinson's poems -- I won't quote them here. It strikes me that they're so personal that I can't share them even with you, my good doctor. But suffice to say, she found her way out from darkened rooms and from behind closed doors through poetry.

Wednesday, February 16, 1994

Tonight we celebrated our 25th wedding anniversary with Chinese take-out and a very good bottle of Moet Chandon that I'd tucked away for just such an occasion. Sam brought me a bouquet of flowers. It has its traditions, this marriage.

Today was my first day back at work after the "petite crisis" and I was resolute about not hiding my illness. I'd made up my mind to be absolutely candid with my co-workers and, of course, it was unnecessary. The world doesn't revolve around me, eh, cher ami?!! And people are politely discreet.

You have been very, very helpful in the past few days. And courageous. Bravo, mon medecin bon.

Jusqu'a Lundi, I am, somewhat precariously,

Moi-meme, sain et sauf

Jess

Tuesday, February 22, 1994

Cher ebon ami,

I woke early this morning, my mind filled with thoughts suggested by our last session. We covered a good deal of ground despite being handicapped by the external realities of my illness.

We spoke about avoidant and excitory behaviors. About monotheism. We spoke of what's fictional and what's real in an interactive therapeutic relationship. And all of this was tremendously helpful to me. Still I woke early this morning from a restful sleep and was reluctant to do what was most natural--write a few pages, take a hot bath perhaps--since these acts might be construed as aberrant behavior in my house. You see, I still fear this, even though the last two weeks haven't borne out this conclusion--that I'm insane and it's my insanity that's causing all the trouble within our family. It's true, however, that until now I've acceded to being the designated "fou."

Ah, the steam begins to come up now and I'm on a favorite couch, wrapped in afghans, seduced by the comfort of my possessions. These are things I wouldn't have had in the hospital. I would have to beg for my perfume bottle, negotiate for a hair dryer. The loss of personal freedom is greater than the benefit to me at this point.

Wednesday, February 23, 1994

Dear friend, I'm feeling much better on this new medication. I have "myself, safe and sane" again. But Mimi's had a conference with a counselor at school and she's been referred for psychiatric help. She's scared and depressed and alone all at the same time. I've been keeping in close contact with her and trying to stay calm through her crisis. We've decided not to tell Sam just yet. But Cara is aware and will be strong for her if she needs a sisterly shoulder. Actually I'm less upset than I would ordinarily be. It's not simply my defense mechanism, which I have termed "desensitization," working—Mimi confirms what I've known for a long time, and never confronted—that she'll inevitably need to deal with certain issues and that in the resolution of these issues she may be able to free herself from the past and make a future separate from us. The result of crisis is conflict resolution.

You should know that I'm considerably more focused and feeling physically much better these last two days. We seem to have pulled me through this latest break. If I were to criticize anybody it would be myself, for taking life too seriously.

This from a recent magazine ad:

> Why does the world automatically get so serious when you grow up? Aren't there still strawberries to be stolen? Lakes to skinny dip in? Cigars to smoke? Waiters to flirt shamelessly with? When exercised regularly, your funny bone's the last to go.

I admit without shame and with some pride to having done all of the above, including smoking a cigar! And now I creep around my own house in fear...in fear of what? *That*, my friend, is something we should explore. Jusqu'a Lundi, I'm once again,

Moi-meme, sain et sauf

Jess

I'd snapped back quickly and without having to be hospitalized. It was a victory of sorts. Dr. Bernard was pleased with himself, I could tell, for having acted to dispel any doubts I might have had about his professional competency until this point. We'd been tested and we were bound together in an unspoken trust by the experience. What I didn't know was that Sam, stung by exclusion, had written Bernard an unpleasant letter, complaining about how he'd handled this setback. This was only the beginning of a tension between them that was destined to destroy much of what was positive in the therapy. In the meantime, I continued the letters despite my intention to push for a completely face -to-face situation.

Wednesday evening, March 2, 1994

Cher ebon ami,

We're very pleased with ourselves, you and I, for having gotten through a crisis time. We sit and grin at each other like two children who've had an adventure! Nevertheless, I feel compelled to make some additional comments about our last session--as usual, I'm querulous and argumentative, but as I told you, it's only because I admire your mind and feel that you're always equal to my arguments.

I'm somewhat puzzled by your passive acceptance of other people's biases. You'd let them pass, sit quietly while irrational and illogical remarks were made about your race. There's something in it, something self-preserving and protective, perhaps, like water rolling off a duck's back, but it isn't social conscience. And I do have a social conscience. Certainly it's been repressed and suppressed for the greater part of my adult life, but I long for social justice and chafe at the injustices I see perpetrated by fear and ignorance. I'm also a pacifist, for the most part. Sometimes I think it all started with my not being able to tolerate loud noise when I was a child. I still can't stand loud noise. That's why Sam's yelling and screaming is such a punishment to me.

I must admit, however, that when I first became involved with feminism, I too glorified motherhood just as you were about to do when you spoke about the biological differences between men and women. So I appreciate the elegant praise you were about to give my sex, but you've touched on the controversial issue of essentialism, I think. Since you won't read my thesis, I will read to you from it...Ruth Bleier in her book *Science and Gender: A Critique of Biology and its Theories on Women,* 1984, wrote the following:

> ...it is important to see that unlike breathing...the biological capacity to reproduce does not necessarily mean that one <u>has</u> to reproduce or even be heterosexually active, nor does it dictate the social

80

arrangements for child nurturance and rearing or determine how child rearing affects one's participation in other cultural activities. Whether or not we bear, nurse, or mother children is just as much a function of cultural, social, political, economical, and no more importantly, biological factors as whether we are poets or soccer players.

Bleier defined essentialist thinking as "a belief in the existence of an ultimate essence within each of us that does not change,' adding that this belief has "always functioned as a central feature of ideologies of oppression." I'm a good mother because I'm a conscientious human being and because I've found a great deal of self-definition in raising my children. I'm not all that enamored of the actual birth process as some women are, but I do feel that having children was the most creative thing I've done in my life. However, I viewed the care of my children as my *choice*, not my duty. It required a certain kind of alertness and intuition that I found exciting. The only thing I regret is that I gave myself over so completely to living life vicariously through Jane. She was so open to it and it was a perfect role for one who enjoys living on the margin.

So, my dear friend, yes, I do believe in biological differences between men and women, but I don't believe that they are so pronounced as some would have us believe. I question where that line of thought leads. I'm not an earth mother, a goddess, nor am I a cyborg or a slave. I'm simply a woman with many dimensions. And you're not a god, although just lately, I'm liable to think of you as one, since your protection has been as if I'm in strong hands at all times, powerful and sure.

As for your remark that I use projective identification, that I project onto the other person, make them miserable and then identify with them, I categorically deny it. In the past, we discussed ego diffusion, a giving up of self to something greater than self. Why do you insist upon reducing me to the sterile jargon of your profession? And such pejorative phrases at that! Let me hear instead about emotions. About fear, worry, despair, hope, dreams, passion, ecstasy. By the way, I can't write five sentences in French as you asked me to do. French is too passionate, too intimate a language. I find that I don't want to make innocuous statements in French. Jusqu'a Lundi, cher medecin, tu me manques. You see!

Moi-meme, sain et sauf

Jess

He'd tried to praise me by flattering my motherhood. Even though I knew it was genuine praise on his part, it opened into one of the feminist issues -- essentialism -- that I had until now avoided thinking about. For the first time, I wrote freely about it. I'd come a long way from my original halting steps, doubts and fears about being understood by this man. And I recalled that at one of our first meetings, he'd exhibited all the reservations and skepticism that some thinking men continue to harbor about gender issues. Feminism? What is it? Why even bother? Where's the need?

In the meantime, he'd brought his strongest yet indictment against me -- projective identification he called it. Was I in fact spreading some sort of miasma of misery to others and then identifying with them in their consequent state of unhappiness? How could I have such a powerful effect? I didn't view my own condition or situation as miserable, only terribly difficult -- it was true I showed little outward emotion, but the idea of projecting misery on others was a far too aggressive one. People, it seemed to me, wanted nothing more than to be understood, heard out fully and then understood. And there was little that couldn't be worked out that way. My faith, what little I continued to have, lay in making that empathic connection, that humane leap to meet the other, hear them out, relate my own experience to what I'd heard.

Tuesday evening, March 8, 1994

Cher ebon ami,

I think I will die of existential boredom as you described it, punctuated only by sporadic anger and despair at my circumstances — the only way I know I'm alive these days. My life is only repetition, with the exception of the pitched battles I have with "mon mari." I have nothing to look forward to, except an hour with you on Monday. And you'll excuse me if that isn't enough. In the meantime, I take my medicine like a good girl and hang on to bits and pieces of scattered optimism. For example, Sam will play a hotel in the Catskills this summer. He will also be performing there the week of Passover. Since I'm off for Good Friday, I'll join him there the Thursday evening before and be able to have two whole days up in the country. Escape! My acceptable escapes grow fewer and fewer.

You know I was very envious of you when you described your passion for long distance driving. At first I felt as if I had nothing comparable in my life. But reading is my adventure and escape. We're a country of movers and travelers—it's one of the ways we overcome class distinctions and avoid categorization. It's a privilege and a freedom, you're right. But for you it's also a delicious physical freedom. Like swimming is for me. It's good to know more about you and how we differ. And you are right, my good doctor, about our commonality—inevitably we do "swim in the same ocean."

You asked me if I'm projecting onto Sam. I think it's just the opposite—he projects himself and his powerless feelings onto me, then gets angry with me and tries even harder to control me. He flies into a rage when I describe a situation at work as if it reflects him. These past few days I've felt more than my share of responsibility for my boss's well being. The rest of the staff inquires about him, not directly to him, you understand, but from me. And his wife even calls and asks me how he is. I've been candid and admitted I don't know how he is—a stroke is such a silent and menacing event. I suppose I'm less apt to say everything is fine, because in my experience it generally isn't.

83

Perhaps I wouldn't feel so responsible for him if I hadn't lost a boss very suddenly over a weekend, years ago. He'd been back from vacation only a week and he was tan and looking very fit but he complained of a problem with his arm and said he was going to see an orthopedist about it. We said goodnight and the next day someone from the office called me to say he'd driven himself to the hospital and had a massive heart attack in the emergency room. Dead. And I was given the task as his secretary of emptying out his briefcase.

Somehow the bad memories begin to drown out the good ones. I really feel that it's my true nature to be hopeful, but events have a way of overtaking me and I'm overwhelmed by the task of "making lemonade out of the lemons life gives me." Only you refuse to see me as negative and self-pitying, only you see me as triumphing over adversities. Why is that so, cher ami?

Last evening I slept soundly and easily after our session. I simply must carve more time out for myself, away from the demands of others, even those who love me. I need to relax and process some of the things I'm only sensing these days. I need to free up my mind from its prison. Like getting in a car and driving straight through....

Wednesday evening, March 9, 1994

I'm feeling a little better this evening. Must be because I got paid today. Compensation. But also because the boss is understanding and sympathetic. He called me in today and had a talk with me about what's happened and my feelings about it. He genuinely cares.

I think there are two themes that run through this past week. Expectations. My own and those of others. I have a tendency to expect too much from myself and too much from others in close situations. And coping mechanisms. I can't simply rely on a pill to do the entire job for me. As a family we have no management systems for stressful, problematic situations. Therefore, I'm faced with the lonely task of developing effective coping mechanisms.

Let me quote to you from an article written by Alfred Kazin I read this week in **The New Yorker**—he began the article this way:

> In the midst of death we are in life--and
> itching to get away for the weekend

And about science and literature, he writes:

> Science, seeking confirmation, proof, and objective testing, cannot avail itself of this cardinal human loneliness, but literature can. And this with language that is always failing and stumbling, breaking the writer's heart with its mere approximateness to the thing in his mind. Besides, language is always asserting its primitive authority—is a halting servant but can be a terrible master. Science progresses all the time, literature never. How should it "improve" over the centuries when its very subject is the enigma, the inaccessibility of the human condition.

I can't write to you in French as you wish, because I won't risk writing in baby talk and that's what I'd have to do to construct the five sentences. At times, my mother tongue is all I have of mother and the only way I know I had a father. Jusqu'a Lundi, nous prenons le meme chemin.

Moi-meme, sain et sauf

Jess

What I really desired, I think, was to ensure that he was, as the reader of the letters, my accomplice. This was my aim, rather than projective identification, an awful sounding term and accusatory as well. But accomplice -- well that fairly reverberated with nuances. My accomplice was as much implicated as I was, as much invested in the outcome. My accomplice was a willing listener, who followed my lead no

85

matter how many tortuous turns my thinking took, no matter how out of the way, how marginal it became. My accomplice moved with me, changed with me, planned with me in the face of fate and arbitrary events. I thought of my shadow, how aware of it I'd been as a little girl. And then I thought of my brother.

He was two and a half years older than me and he'd been my hero for as long as I could remember. A skinny, energetic kid with a shock of chestnut hair, quick witted and possessing that certain bravado that goes with being born male into a world where everything seemed possible.

He had courage and imagination. He was forever making plans, dreaming dreams, scheming with a certain combination of purpose and optimism that was irresistible to me. I followed him everywhere. With my first few pennies, I went to the dimestore and bought miniature cars and trucks for him. It seemed to me that he made things happen. We had, after all, won the war. Thom, born in 1939, was, at seven or eight years old, emblematic of those qualities that had to come to the fore to make that happen -- a certain naive enthusiasm for the great enterprise that was life, a cheerful determination. He had a way of organizing our little ragtag bunch of neighborhood kids, of galvanizing our play so that it bespoke its own narrative. Our days had a beginning, middle and an end with Thom's genius for crafting them. Our play was charged with meaning, meaning that mostly came from his inventiveness.

His features were small, delicate, fine boned. There was a chiseled look to the nose and chin. He had small ears and a well-shaped head. His upper teeth slightly protruded, an overbite, they called it. In later years, his mouth would take on a set grimace, drawn over his teeth, as if he were in pain. Perhaps he was...but that was later. But then, he was a boy with an ingenuous grin on a face lifted toward the camera, squinting into the sun, his arm around his best friend, the baker's son -- he resembled my mother's mother then. I think it was his sense of himself as free, a totally free agent, author of his own life that drew us all to him. And we were drawn to him. That's why it came as such a shock when he told me I couldn't come with him and his friends any more. I was seven then, he was nine. Until that time, he'd always included me, taken me with him to the movies. But now I'd become a burden. I was just a girl and a younger one at that, totally useless. Useless for what? Why? I couldn't understand this sudden complete rejection by the most important person in my life. On Saturdays, I took to going to the movies on my own. Or I'd read. I began to devour books as if they were hot fudge sundaes. Every week or so, I'd drop in at the bookstore to see if they'd gotten any new books in -- I'd begun to collect them in orange crate book cases. I was intensely lonely. The year before we'd left the bar, the neighborhood, my friends and my father and gone to live with my mother's father up near the lake. I was in a different school, certainly a different world and my brother had decentered it by excluding me from his circle.

Tuesday evening, March 15, 1994

Cher ebon ami,

I must confess I painted too bleak a picture last evening, although my purpose was to share what has come to be my reality with you. Still, I didn't want to make you feel powerless to help me--I know what that feels like. I think you're the greatest help by providing some continuity in an otherwise dissociate life. Right now, I think we are both concerned and probably a bit ill at ease with where all this is going to lead. To ease your mind, mon cher medecin, no, I don't feel unhappy all week long. I have my moments, but then I'm so sensitive to people and sun and air and weather, to the perverse and unexpected, to the many possibilities, and I'm very curious...I think this is merely the aftermath of a crisis intervention--the peeling of my eyes to "what is" and I also mourn every spring for a really wonderful past. You see, it's not death I celebrate, but the richness of relationships that have slipped away and that I haven't been able to replace. And so, the tulips I chose yesterday for my office were a wonderful soft purple color. I love them, with their large fleshy leaves and black furry stamens. Purple, like big soft purple hearts, instead of the usual banal

87

pastels that herald spring. I haven't the courage to believe in rebirth—that's why the spring holds little promise for me.

You spoke of a "psychology of empowerment." I think it masks your impatience with me. I've always doubted whether you have the patience to work things through in a different way--without tinkering with my mind as if I was something to be fixed like a machine. When you try to persuade me to be more like you, you're asking the impossible, my friend. I can't model myself after you, nor would you want me to if you took a good look into your soul. Yes, I must love myself, but I must first accept a whole self. As for you, first you must *love my sadness*. It's an honorable grief in a good cause. And then perhaps, just perhaps I'll learn how to be more like "moi-meme," that whole, authentic, self-assured adult woman that I aspire to be at the end of each letter. Remember, your personal goals for me aren't necessarily the goals I set for myself. Don't be misled because I write that I envy you. I do not want to *be* you. You are a good soul to want to share the thrill of physical freedom with me, but that's not possible. And that's what I tried to point out to you during our last session. Your compassion, however, overtakes us both.

It matters much more to me that I have something I've written published than it does to be able to drive a car. You see, although I'm at present confronted with too few avenues of escape, I'm painfully aware that when I do escape, I must always return to immutable, unchanging sameness. The only thing that has changed that to any extent in the last several years is achievement and recognition. Applause, my good and dear friend. I'm not ashamed to say it to you. Right now, my struggle is with an unendurable private life and a responsible public life. I'm infinitely more comfortable in public (though you are right--I'm plagued by a performance anxiety). I come home to a very sad and silent house. Only the possibility of seeing you each week lessens that struggle.

Last evening, after our session, I called my friend and confidante, Lenny. I suppose I'm letting the cat out of the bag, but I have to confess that the two things I do almost ritualistically after our session is eat ice cream and talk to Lenny.

We spoke about the value of fantasy, its healthful properties. Lately, my tendency is to suppress fantasy and pleasurable experiences as a sort of self-correction. And yet I'm not facing up to the enormous frustrations in my life. But getting back to fantasy.

For instance, I'm very much looking forward to the opportunity to attend the lecture being given by Saul Bellow this coming Monday evening. I daydream about speaking to him, telling him about the paper I'm writing about him, asking him all the questions that occur to me while I'm writing. And in my dream, he finds in me a new interest, a renewed energy. We share Chicago as our common background, a deep and abiding interest in the psychology of place belongingness. And suddenly, in my fantasy, I'm able to speak in a voice, not completely unknown to me, but rarified and authorial. For once I own my words. Then I shake myself back to reality—I'll be attending only to listen, a member of an anonymous audience. I feel unable to compose even one suitable question for the question and answer period to follow the lecture. But this isn't a new fantasy. The more I read, the more I want to engage the authors in conversation. When I'm actually offered the opportunity I stammer and gush and leave feeling empty and unsatisfied. Words have been subverted by overwhelming admiration. Celebrity has cowed me and I'm reduced to a blushing, stammering schoolgirl.

I believe we've come to some sort of impasse in the therapy, you and I--the more important you become to me, the more I believe you will abandon me (or should abandon me). I doubt my ability to hold your interest; I doubt your ability to remain faithful to our alliance. Did you notice at our last session how each of us punished the other in our dream life. Perhaps we're about to enter a new phase.

Wednesday, March 16, 1994

I came home tonight to what I thought might be an answer from my mentor, about publishing the letters. It was instead a subscription renewal to his poetry journal. I haven't the courage to call him. I've imagined his rejection of my work a hundred different ways. And today, ironically, my boss told me he thinks I'm doing much better. Of course, I'm simply muddling through in my estimation. And will continue to, jusqu'a Lundi (at 6:30!)

Moi-meme, sain et sauf

Jess

By this time, the letters were beginning to look like a book to me. True they were raw, unedited, almost encrypted, but reading them back I was moved by my laid bare soul. They did, however, have parameters. It wasn't a dialogue. No, it was more like speaking to an idealized version of self, the lover we all dream of having, the Other — it was subject speaking to object. Our alliance nevertheless, was a catalyst and ideas, issues and memories that had been formless, now took shape.

Tuesday evening, March 22, 1994

Cher ebon ami,

I thought we had one of our better sessions last evening. I was particularly pleased about the sanction you put on me to "hold" some of your thoughts and ideas—generally I'm too quick to respond and since we live in a world of sound bytes, I welcome the chance to think through some of what you suggest to me.

It seems as though we are "deconstructing" what had become, over time, an inflated diagnosis by closely examining the structure of its parts. What we're doing is a lively and spirited redefinition. I like to think that I help in this project by spurring you to think about received definitions, to develop a different perspective and shake off the sterile determinants of your (thank God!) inexact science. For just as you reject the voodoo mythology that surrounds death in your culture and create instead your own illusion about death (swift and sure and imperious, like the dark silhouette in <u>Amadeus</u>) I reject the mythology of the helping profession and the psychobabble that so permeates it and instead envision the creation of a simple, vigorous, totemic, all-inclusive psychology anchored in the infinite and forgiving nuances of language. How I loved to hear you say that rather than use the wrong word, you would make up a word to satisfy the demands of meaning! (As for me, I think that death is small and ignominious--life, only life looms large. That's my illusion.)

For the first time, I almost wished I'd caught you on tape— particularly your thoughts on "self definition" and its limitations. But if I can't catch your spoken thoughts out of the air in my fist, then I'll have to trust to the providence of consciousness, won't I. And speaking of consciousness that's what the lecture last night was mostly about.

Bellow is old and beyond redemption, I'm afraid. He's returned to the safe harbor of academia to die. Many times before, he had delivered distinctly anti-academic lectures, valiantly defended imagination, and remained aloof and apart. But last night, he was like an aging prostitute, unsure of what he had to give, unsure of what was wanted of him—only interested in getting paid. I know the academic community where he lectured fairly well. They'd probably used him up during the reception and the dinner that preceded the lecture. He'd been persuaded to scrap some fifteen pages of a prepared manuscript, speak for about twenty minutes and then open it up to a "dialogue" with his audience. Unfortunately, the audience was a particularly innocuous and obedient one. And so, he read from what had probably been a grand piece of writing, but which was chopped up so much he could hardly follow his own thoughts. What a shame. I felt like asking him for the parts he'd left out so that I could read them in the privacy of my study.

Interestingly, Sam asked me about the lecture in the car this morning on the way to the station. When I told him how disappointed I was and how Bellow, who's teaching a course on contemporary writers at Boston University, mentioned the names of many young writers but that there was not one woman among the lot, how when he was asked to name the writers of his generation he thought promising, he named only men, how totally excluded women in general were from his remarks, his reminiscences, Sam asked if I intended to go forward with the paper on Bellow. How strange and thrilling it felt to be asked that question. He never acknowledges my writing.

Wednesday evening, March 23, 1994

What a glorious day! 68 degrees! I took a long walk at lunchtime today and what a struggle it was to return to my office. Sam's working tonight. I like it when he works. Reminds me of other times in our life. And it gives me some much-needed time to myself. I'm having my business partners over for dinner on Friday evening. We're taking in a friend to sell our services this spring. We have high hopes for our little editorial design business. Lenny feels ready to take on more business. So I prepared ahead of time, made out my bills, finished this letter to you. While I was washing up in the kitchen, I suddenly thought of the time I spoke to you on the phone and you asked if I'd gone into work that day. There was an implied parallel—we'd both had to work. If felt so good. Like two horses in their traces, separate, but pulling together. So in a way I've gotten my wish after all. Of my four men, three are willing and able to work alongside me. Oh, cher ami, je suis heureuse ce soir. My boss wants me to tell you that he's noticed a change for the better in my attitude at work. Whatever we're doing, it's working!

I continue to confront those tasks I'd ordinarily avoid for whatever reason--because I'm too shy or because I don't like to ask for money, or because some problems look insurmountable. And each time I tackle some knotty little problem, I feel so energized, so encouraged. When I look back on the last month or two, I can hardly believe I made it through with heart to spare and soul to keep. I'm so looking forward to seeing you this week. Things are looking up!

Moi-meme, sain et sauf

Once more I'd pulled out of a depressive break and was on the mend. The deepest part of that terrible winter was over. I longed for the reconciliation of summer all that long raw spring. He continued to urge me to write the letters.

Tuesday evening, March 29, 1994

Cher ebon ami,

So, you'd like to be invisible and watch me while I write my letters! Sir, that's the beauty of the letters—they're utterly a personal and private creation. They're something that happens between me and a blank screen, something whimsical, yet powerful, an occurrence that transcends the everyday, transports me to another world where I'm the sole originator of the body and breadth of every page. Of course, the letters must have a destination and a willing recipient. That's where you come in, my would-be voyeur. Once again, you wish emotional proof of the existence of a true, embodied voice. Suffice to say, I write the letters in a little room under the eaves, surrounded by the past, by my books and papers, with a portable radio playing classical music in the background. Classical music keeps my mind lively and, I believe, regulates the heart.

I slept last night to the steady drumbeat of spring rain against the bedroom window. It's only one of the things that make me happy these days. But how can I explain what makes me happy—they're such incidental things. The light on the side of a whitewashed building, the cast of certain skies, or a soft, soaking rain. The lightness of my clothes, the ease with which I walk to the train in the evening. The light, the light, the light. The sound of a friendly voice on the phone, of a Strauss waltz or Gershwin's *Rhapsody in Blue* on my radio on the train ride home, the easy talk I overhear in restaurants or on the street as I move invisibly among strangers. Light and sound make me happy. Don't you see? I've allowed the prisoner clemency. For, as someone once said, just as nothing can stay good forever, nothing can stay bad forever either. Sooner or later something's got to give, as they say in the song. This time it's me. It occurs to me that perhaps I've made too much of duty and honor-bound conscience in these letters to you. I've worried that you would find me lacking in moral sensibilities and not take me seriously. These qualities, after all, are rarely ascribed to women.

What you said in closing at our last session proves you undiscerning, but it doesn't mean you are indifferent to injustice, I hope. Since you were so long an innocent in the Garden of Eden that was Haiti, I would guess that in your old age, you'll return to the innocent exuberance of your youth. People usually do. I can hardly believe that you'll be satisfied with so taciturn a pastime as fishing, and certainly you won't have that sly smirk of guilty satisfaction that your statue of the old reprobate fisherman has—he strikes me as a man of the world, who's kicked over his traces only after having his fill of hell raising—he's hardly, nor was he ever, I surmise, innocent. And I think that you love fast cars, good clothes and high culture too much to ever go "naturelle" like him. Is it really the simple life you yearn for? Are you really so undiscerning, so completely without value judgments as your protestations would have me believe?

As for me, I understand oppression and exclusion too well to claim that I don't care. However, I seem hell bent on impressing you with those facts until you're dismayed at my occasional happy moment. Monsieur, even a slave's heart knows joy sometimes, even if it's only an illusion with which she's set herself free. Let's say that this last week's events and the major players in my life have conspired to make that illusion seem more real. Of course, this is about control, reclaiming control in the face of an absurd and arbitrary existence.

Thus far, you've confessed to me all the things you don't care about in life, cher ami. According to your account, you're an atheist, who cares little for the traditions and trappings of religion, you're apolitical and indifferent to social inequities and racial discrimination, ignorant of the basic differences among religions and ethnic groups, and supremely pragmatic. "If it feels good, go with it, if it feels bad, pay no attention." I ask myself, why then do I seek my cure with you? The answer is I seek an ethical impartial therapy and literary inspiration and I've found both these last several months with you. The letters are my cure and your appetite for them is the key to our relationship. You have the perfect combination of interest and indifference to be my universal reader. You reflect the content of the letters in our talks by telling me about yourself, by sitting outside of the charmed circle of authority where, as my doctor, you might impose your will upon me, and by offering yourself unstintingly.

You know, when I was in the hospital last May, there was a woman who'd come in from a shelter for the homeless. She was wildly mad and heavily medicated and unaware of most of what went on around her. She confined herself to the kitchen area mostly where she spoke in a loud voice without inflection and told her story in rough street language to anyone who would listen. Of course, she was never satisfied with anyone's response, but she made me uncomfortably aware of the limitations of language to describe real feelings. Over and over to anyone who would listen, she'd say, "Hey, I've been goosed by a three hundred pound man!" Everyone heard her, but few stopped to consider what she must feel, even if what she claimed had happened had only happened in her mind. I used to think about it a lot. Like the others, I had no answer for her, no way to make it up to her. But I knew at some level what it is to accept that indignity and to continue. Maybe imagination is necessary in order to have a social conscience.

Let me tell you what I know about odd combinations, for we're most certainly an odd combination, you and I. Odd combinations as part of proteanism are a way of dealing with the sequential nature of modern life. In Lifton's new book *The Protean Self: Human Resilience in an Age of Fragmentation*, he writes:

> The essence of the protean self lies in its odd combinations. There is a linking--often loose but functional--of identity elements and subselves not ordinarily associated with one another to the point of even seeming..."mutually irreconcilable." The new combinations may take one in unexpected directions and provide one with equally unexpected capacities.

Lifton quotes from Salman Rushdie, "How does newness come into the world? How is it born? Of what fusions, translations, conjoinings is it made: How does it survive, extreme and dangerous as it is?"

Finally, Lifton writes:

> Rushdie flies the protean banner in declaring that *Satanic Verses* "celebrates hybridity, impurity, intermingling, the transformation that comes of new and unexpected combinations of human beings, cultures, ideas, politics, movies, songs. It rejoices in the mongrelisation and fears the absolutism of the Pure." ... What is gained by this "postmodern prophet of the confluence of cultures" is the imaginative power--and the importance for all of us--of the new combinations achieved.

And that's what I know about odd combinations. I'm joining Sam in the mountains on Thursday evening and hope to spend some relaxed and productive time there. He tells me that we have a very nice room that overlooks a wood. He would be delighted if you and your wife would care to hear him play at a jazz brunch he does every Sunday in the city from 11 to 3 pm. There's a good singer and the crowd seems to enjoy the brunch very much. It's a nice setting and I think you might enjoy it.

I look forward to seeing you again on Monday. Stay bright and beautiful, my good doctor.

Moi-meme, sain et sauf

Jess

He'd asked whether Sam was good at what he did. There was the usual confusion between performance and talent, the latter grounded only in the discipline of music, the former requiring an audience and an invitation. The phone rarely rang to invite Sam to play anymore — there were few invitations to show off his talent. It was a raw, unformed, uncultivated talent -- one simply sat him at a piano and he played.

My mind was still blown with residual terrors and intrusive thoughts. I welcomed the slow rhythms and the impersonal nature of the hotel where Sam was going to play. I craved retreat and anonymity.

Saturday afternoon, April 2, 1994

Cher ebon ami,

It's a strange place to retreat to, an old-style Jewish resort hotel in the Catskills, but I must admit that I'm flooded with a host of impressions and observations. It is, of course, an occasion to write to you.

I'm both myself and the Other in this situation — I'm neither hotel guest nor am I part of the myriad network of hotel staff it takes to keep guests happy. I'm an invisible woman, a "private eye" who watches everything and listens to bits and snatches of conversations. Like Bellow's Herzog, "I'm a prisoner of perception, a compulsory witness."

When we drove up in the late afternoon on Thursday, spring thaw was in full tilt, everything was melting, water rushing and spilling over the face of tumbled rock outcroppings, over the black-green sheen of sheared boulders. The sky was awash with gold and ruffled with gray clouds like a pigeon's breast. Up in the mountains, there was still snow on the ground--it was a raw and early spring and here and there locals cautiously moved through the thin spring sunshine as if in a dream.

The hotel is worn and ramshackle, a sprawling maze of added-on buildings connected by a series of impromptu walkways and underground passages. The carpeting is worn and faded and the color scheme is vaguely reminiscent of the 1940s or `50s. There's an outdoor skating rink and a separate building across the road houses indoor tennis courts. There's a huge glassed-in indoor pool, a 9-hole golf course, a card room, a video games room, a theater club, a tea room, a disco, and, of course, a main dining room where guests are plied with gustatory delights and where they can reign like kings and queens at snowy clothed tables beneath crystal chandeliers. Now, at Passover, the guests, in their 70s and 80s, return to celebrate the holiday like salmon instinctively swim upstream to spawn.

Our room, located in an older section of the hotel, a sort of middle class barracks with old rattan furniture in the vestibule, is a mismatch of drapes and bedspreads and electric blue shag carpeting from the 60s, with a sink set up in a cubicle outside the bathroom. It has a double and a single bed, one unbearably unyielding, the other soft and spent. But it's clean and serviceable. Over everything in this place lies the pall of an irretrievable past, of a culture so inured in its rituals and traditions that it can't be replicated, rewritten or reimagined. I look long and hard at the faces of these old people to etch them in my memory—and also because I know I'll travel a similar, if not exactly the same path in old age. Oh, yes, I'll spend it differently, perhaps, but the process will be the same. What, I ask myself, is the secret of their dignity? Of their determination and desire in the face of so much incapacity and constraint? Their limbs are bent, their joints swollen, their backs bowed, their gait slow and uneven, their vision misted over. Yet they carry themselves with purpose, willing participants.

We take our meals in the staff dining room where we sit at one long table and a steady stream of hotel staff, everyone from bellboys to front desk receptionists, masseurs and bookkeepers, security guards, athletic directors, groundspeople, babysitters and other musicians come and go. I'm fascinated by the rigid hierarchy they reflect and enact among themselves and in reaction to the guests they all serve. There's always an electric tension between the servers and the served that's articulated in the back rooms of hotels. My story and my own identity are stretched to their limit here from scrupulous self-examination. Who am I, I ask myself and how do I fit in here?

The indoor pool is heated. Mercifully. I swim every afternoon in warm water and try to remain unobtrusive on my lounge chair which is strategically removed from the action so that I can read and write uninterrupted. The sound of children playing water games in the pool is lively background music. Yesterday I had a massage, the miracle cure for all that ails me after a long, arduous and eventful winter of mental stress and physical inactivity. I contemplate my body in the sauna and the steam room, feeling the perspiration begin to trickle down my back, breathing in the hot, wet steam. I luxuriate in the heat, letting my body finally relax. There's an old woman in the sauna with me. As she rises to leave, I look at her wizened body, breasts like empty pouches lie dispiritedly on her chest, the pelvis tilted stiffly forward, the skin of her thighs withered and sere, large black moles scattered over her back. I think of how the Nazis had carried out their selections, weeding out the old and the infirm. She would have been expendable. But not here. Here she's catered to and cared for. A hotel is not a concentration camp, thank God.

This morning after breakfast I went up to the lounge area outside the tearoom looking for a quiet place to write to you. I was casually dressed and carrying a purse and a carryall bag that held all of my writing materials. I was eager to write to you because the force of my impressions of this new place was pressing me. It was yom tov, the first of the last two days of Pesach and it was also shabbas --services were being held in the theater club and I could hear the cantor and the women of the choir chanting and singing in Hebrew, some of which I remembered from when I was a girl. But here I was most definitely an observer outside the temple. A steady stream of old people were walking past. They were dressed to show respect for the holiday and some, when they heard the cantor's powerful chanting, began to sing the phrases as they walked.

I refrained from writing since I knew it was forbidden on the Sabbath. Instead I read and watched surreptitiously and still they came, physically infirm, ravaged by time and life's blind justice, but they came, in perfect trust, like obedient children. And it occurred to me that I was watching the last of a slightly tarnished, but mostly innocent, generation through a prism of modernity and assimilation, and suddenly I wanted to run away. But I didn't.

They're devoted, yet pragmatic, this group, organized and social. Just the evening before, they'd come to this very same theater club to be entertained by typical "borscht belt" entertainers, who played shamelessly on their "yiddishkeit." They dance the old dances--waltzes, fox trots, tangos, merengues and cha chas. In the afternoons, they gather at tables in the card room to play poker and casino and canasta and pinochle and mah jong, men and women, talking and kibitzing and a freshfaced college boy walks among them pouring from a pitcher of iced water. They sit outside on benches, stiffly bundled in their winter coats in the pale spring sun and talk animatedly to each other for hours. I'm afraid that only cynicism and dissolution and the narcissism of the "me" generation will take their place.

Sam has proved himself these last several nights and the performers as well as the other band members have complimented him. He may do some weekday work at another one of the hotels up here in June and he has a definite commitment to do the summer here.

I hope that you and your family have been well this week. I thought of you often, of course. I wish you a happy holiday in the spirit of rebirth and new life.

Moi-meme, sain et sauf

Jess

Work continued to remain largely a series of empty tasks. My new boss was uncomplicated and easy to work with. I liked his work style. He had a way of including me, getting me involved in what he was working on so that I could find more meaning in the work. He was also dealing with a recalcitrant staff. At times, he'd asked me to come into a meeting that ran through lunch and take their lunch orders. I was chafing at being a waitress for them. I consoled myself by becoming friendlier with the other secretaries, and, at times, I was their spokesperson.

Wednesday, April 6, 1994

Cher ebon ami,

It's no use trying to relate my experiences to you—you're too skeptical, too suspicious. I seek no solace, simply a different perspective. Instead, I get a lot of psychological name-calling and reproof. Why is it so difficult for you to view things from my perspective? Will you become contaminated? Will you dissolve into pieces? Why such resistance to my appeal for good counsel? I can't spend an entire hour fighting to prove that my reality *is* my reality. I'm left spent and exhausted and in the dark. Alone. I would've never thought I would be so alone with you in the same room.

It's a disastrous mistake to hold yourself up as a model for me, to compare my life with yours. There are worlds of difference that must be acknowledged. I'm neither innocent nor ingenuous. I'm intuitive, insightful and thoughtful. Above all, I'm almost painfully honest with you about my perceptions. You deny all of this when you doubt my experience as I tell it to you. Will you be less of a man if you allow yourself to go with my experience of things? I'm not there to sing you to sleep, mon ami. I find you to be most resistant when I exhibit those qualities not generally considered feminine. Ambition, rage, indignation, a desire for visibility and recognition, my own judgment, meeting self-imposed challenges and standards, using strategy. I'm either too "purposeful" or exhibiting a combination of "grandiosity and passivity." Once again you subject me to psychological reductionism and once again I'm found lacking. *I accuse you of having little or no interest in my real life and of being incapable of making that imaginative leap necessary to connect me with my letters.* Quite frankly, I think I'm a better sociologist than you. Katharine Newman in her book *Falling From Grace: Downward Mobility in the Middle Class* writes that,

> People who consider themselves victims of categorical fate are probably the better "social

scientists": They are aware of the ways in which they are perceived by others as exemplars of social groups and are caught up in social processes...which are larger than themselves, while those who see their lives as entirely a matter of individual control are less acute...and tend to overlook the extra-individual factors...

I understand the process whereby a male employer trivializes a job in order to keep a woman's worth within limits. Furthermore, I understand the delicate play of dominance and submission intrinsic to certain work situations. What you describe as your work situation is essentially fraternal. A relationship among three men. I could go on and on, but you choose to deny my assessment of the situation and instead chalk it up to my personal pathology.

Please excuse me if I can't write any more this evening. It seems of no avail. I'll leave you with these thoughts taken from Vivian Gornick's *Essays in Feminism.*

...power and powerlessness are an interlocking two-part fundament permanently associated with the fears and desires of human life, shared by all, yet, in a mythic sense, divided between men and women."

Writers, she says, who wish to write about powerlessness must look for their source to "the femaleness of experience."

...to the idea of the divided psyche; the hesitations of the soul split between being and nonbeing, the complex rather than simple meanings of passivity, the struggle between repressive fears and sympathetic impulses, the awesome power of self-hatred.

I'm having some of the secretaries from my office over to brunch on Sunday. I shall enjoy the sorority of it. Until Monday, then I remain,

Moi-meme, sain et sauf

Jess

We'd reached another impasse. I'd brought him a wounded self and he'd been rough on me. I was profoundly split between my role at work as a secretary and that other subtler self, the writer of the letters, authentic and whole, but only showing itself occasionally, fervent, but frail, and given to abrupt starts and stops. What nerve, I would berate myself, calling yourself a writer when you haven't published a page.

Tuesday evening, April 12, 1994

Cher ebon ami,

I apologize for being so difficult last evening. But conversations like we had are necessary, although painful. Besides, I'm spurred to write to you with even more candor. Tu sais tu remplit ma vie, mon ami. And you can't even remember my age! I would so very much like to be what you wish me to be, but I'm beyond redemption. I wrestle these days with questions and urges. For me spring is no longer about rebirth, but there's still a strong wish for rejuvenation. I long for the happy productive years of the past. It seems I have very little currency to buy my way with these days. I'm more and more aware of the aging process when I look in my mirror. What does one gain when one loses youth, especially a woman?

I know it's spring, because I'm suddenly aware of good looking men on the street. There's something about certain men, a look, a languorous pose that makes me want to take them home to bed with me. I don't wish to speak, only communicate on a level where there is no speech. I want mystery and strong instinctual desire. No roles to play, only surrender and the sheer joy of losing myself in sexual discovery, dissolving in physical pleasure with no regrets and having made no bargains. In my office I have pale lemon yellow freesias and bright starlike tiger lilies this week.

103

I think that my struggle is an attempt to establish my worth in terms of these years. Of everything I said last evening, only one statement rings with satisfactory authority. This is my narrative. You may choose to listen or you may ignore what I'm telling you in my haphazard fashion. *Either way, I'm speaking and writing my life and you are my witness.*

My dear friend, I've been rereading one of my favorite writers, Carolyn Heilbrun.

> And above all other prohibitions, what has been forbidden to women is anger, together with the open admission of the desire for power and control over one's life (which inevitably means accepting some degree of power and control over other lives)...Forbidden anger, women could find no voice in which publicly to complain; they took refuge in depression or madness.

She also writes,

> We women have lived too much with closure:"If he notices me, if I marry him, if I get into college, if I get this work accepted, if I get that job"--there always seems to loom the possibility of something being over, settled, sweeping clear the way for contentment. This is the delusion of a passive life...Safety and closure, which have always been held out to women as the ideals of female destiny, are not places of adventure, or experience, or life. Safety and closure (and enclosure) are rather the mirror of the Lady of Shalott. They forbid life to be experienced directly. Lord Peter Wimsey once said that nine-tenths of chivalry was a desire to have all the fun. The same might be said of patriarchy.

How I wish I had the courage to step out in a different direction, mon ami. I'm certain that life has more to offer than I know right now. It's risky business this therapy. Please remember that a gentle prescriptive has far more value than a corrective one in my case. You allow me little room of my own.

But I chalk it up to your youth and life experience and your immersion in the culture of self-improvement. Dorothy Sayer's female detective, Harriet Vane wrote these words: "the best remedy for a bruised heart is not, as so many people seem to think, repose upon a manly bosom. Much more efficacious are honest work, physical activity, and the sudden acquisition of wealth." Ce n'est pas drole?

Since I've been writing to you, I've neglected so many other correspondences, so much of the post graduate research and writing I aspired to....there are so many subjects we could talk about if only you weren't intent on "curing" me. For just as the staff in the hospital didn't "kill me or cure me," this therapy which staggers drunkenly along, trying to fit my formidable self within the recipes and panaceas drawn from your good heart, will not do more. Loosen up, mon medecin bon, and I will tell you 1,000 stories from the Arabian nights that is my "bruised heart."

> Women will starve in silence until new stories
> are created which confer on them the power of
> naming themselves.
> Stanley Cavell
> *Pursuits of Happiness*

Jess

Tuesday evening, April 19, 1994

Cher ebon ami,

It's a delightful little charade we play when you leave your door ajar, as you did at our last session, and I descend to find you seated at your desk for all the world like a psychologue serieuse. It reminds me of child's play--of hide and seek. I should always like to discover you unaware, off guard and slightly distracted. And instead of expecting me, I'd like you to be suddenly surprised by my presence. In a way, I'd like my entire life to be like that—a series of chance encounters, like the "joyful collisions" of Frank Gehry's architecture. As I grow old and move inexorably along on the continuum of time, more and more I wish for spontaneity, not certitude. You're right, I do suffer from too much certitude. I crave distraction, an unplanned day, an unexpected meeting, an unpredictable conversation, original thoughts. I should like my heart to leap at the sight of someone....

Ah, 'bon ami, here's the paradox—that, I, who has always suffered a delay in affect, who hides behind a cultivated and calculated reserve and waits to be discovered, should wish for uncalculated and immediate response from others. I'm once again confronted by my own defection. It's when I look at you that I see myself as disingenuous. For despite your practiced indifference to my interpretation, you're never any more or less than you claim to be. And this is what I value of you.

Outside my window, I hear the roll of thunder and lightning streaks light up the spring night. I love spring thunderstorms, especially those threatening moments before the rain comes.

Since you told me two stories from your school days, I will tell you several of my own. It was the summer after high school graduation and I'd taken the state scholarship exam. I flew through the part of the exam that dealt with language, but then there was the math section. I was hopelessly lost. I didn't even know what to write on the scratch pad they'd given us. Afterwards, when the scholarships were returned by those who were planning to go to school out of state, I was notified that I'd qualified as a recipient. During that hot, still summer, my mother told me it wouldn't be possible for me to go to college.

I'd never felt myself to be a particularly powerful member of my family. For years, I'd felt like so much baggage that my mother carried around from place to place. Children and pets. Landlords and superintendents viewed my brother and me as inconvenient, neighbors were either distant or complained about us if we made noise. As a teenager, I'd felt insignificant and uncomfortable beneath the gaze of these authority figures.

But that summer, I grabbed for the big brass ring, a ticket out of isolation and mediocrity. I went to see my mother's former lover, a confirmed bachelor who sat every evening and drank himself into oblivion in the Commonwealth Lounge on the corner of Diversey and Pine Grove, only down the block from where we lived. It was a favorite hangout for mafia types, their women and an assortment of sub rosa con artists and "carny" types.

Charlie G., a respectable Jewish businessman, lived with his mother in stately rooms on Lake Shore Drive, the area known as the "Gold Coast" that ran along the Chicago lakefront. He'd had a series of girlfriends. My mother was the last in a distinguished line of bleached blondes who he'd "kept,"—that was how it was referred to in those days, the habit of making a long term sexual bargain—not lavishly, but in rent and shoes and the necessities. The difference between my mother and her predecessors being that she was from a good family, a family that had achieved some prominence in Chicago.

When I went to Charlie to ask for the money to go to school, my mother had been married to someone else for two years. I was sixteen when I came home from high school one day to find several suitcases and a case holding an army medal sitting in the middle of the living room. That's how I met my mother's second husband. They came in that evening and announced they were married. Now, two years later and without the benefit of my mother's sexual bargain as leverage, I approached this gruff, little man who'd kept her as a chatelaine since I was eight years old and I asked him to send me to college. And he did. Not only did he pay my room and board (my scholarship covered tuition and fees), but every time I dropped him a note, he sent me spending money. To this day, I don't know where I got the courage, the temerity to ask or what his motives were for sending me. But I maintained good grades and my scholarship was renewed every year that I was at school. So rare are the times I've taken my destiny in my own hands. So rare.

The first thing I knew at college was that everything I knew up until then no longer applied. One class stays in my mind. It was my habit by the time I was in my sophomore year to sit in the back of the classroom by myself. I liked to hold myself apart from the rest of my classmates as a sign of my individualism. It

107

was the first day of the semester and the subject was literature. We'd been waiting for the professor for some time, when a man who looked like the janitor strode up to the front and took his place at the podium. I couldn't believe by the look of him that this was to be our professor. Not only had I been downstaged as the lone individual, but I would find few who would match his wit and intelligence then or in the years to come. We read *Crime and Punishment* that semester. I remember reading it in a Russian fever and loving it. There wasn't a mark on the paper I wrote for him, except at the very bottom of the last page where he had written simply "thank you."

By the end of my sophomore year, I was involved with a faculty member from the English Department. He was a man in his forties who was something of a cult figure to his students. I would spend a lot of time at his house, listening to his record collection and browsing through his books. His friends were much older than I and a good deal more sophisticated. His wife, who was a beauty, had only recently left him. He treated me as if I was some fascinating and rare creature. And, in a way, I suppose I was--somewhere between acquisitive teenager and young woman. He failed, however, to take my virginity, which was becoming increasingly burdensome to me.

So, my beautiful listener, my college career was destined to end abruptly and in shame, but it was not without its enchantments and accomplishments, its gentle unfolding and rare moments. Tu me manque ce soir.

I'll leave you with some interesting quotes from *Multiplicity of Dreams: Memory, Imagination and Consciousness* by Harry T. Hunt. Mr. Hunt writes that "it is never clear in the human sciences whether we lead society to new discoveries or are merely led in turn by its pervasive ideologies of power and order."

He also says (and I think we would both agree):

All human reality can be taken twice over, in terms of meaning and cause, subject and object. The subject-object division itself and the postmodern realization of our inherent relativity and perspectivism guarantees that any foreseeable science of human beings will be perpetually two-sided.

And with this final thought, I will leave you for my pillow, while the thunder still rolls outside my window. Hunt writes that "In psychology we attempt a science...of material that is classically expressed in mythology and the arts." The key word is expressed, don't you think? It is expressivity that matters, don't you agree?

Jusqu'a Lundi, then I'm

moi-meme, sain et sauf

Jess

Two years after Janie died, I'd managed to land a job at the local university where I was completing my bachelor's degree in humanities. It had required that I take a cut in pay, but the opportunity it provided to work and attend school in the same place, continually immersed, I thought, in the heady ideas of academia, was irresistible to me. I finished up my bachelor's degree while I worked as part of the university's public relations department. It was like a dream. Every day I walked into one of the main buildings on campus, in fact it was the building where the President's office was located, and took my place, true it was as a lowly assistant, with the four other women who made up the department. I did any and all the tasks they gave me only too gladly. I was learning how things worked in public relations, picking it up like a sponge, working as an apprentice to some very talented and politically savvy women. And then the axe fell. The President sacked the head of our department, a petite blonde from Barnard with a terrible scar on one side of her face from a botched attempt to surgically remove a disfiguring port wine stain. She was smart and sophisticated, a p.r. strategist who could hold her own with any in the private sector. At first I'd been intimidated by her, but then we'd buckled down and worked, all of us, hard, and she'd warmed to the task and I found that I admired how she handled us. In any event, it was all over before I could write my first press release. She was fired and the administration was after the two writers just below her. I was advised to run before they got to me. Word had it they were looking to wipe the slate clean and start again.

I sought protection on the other side of the campus in the office of the deposed dean of the school of social work. He'd been banished to an obscure office in an intellectual cul de sac, a tony private school that shared the campus grounds. From that vantage point and somewhat pacified by his elite title, he taught several graduate level courses in social work and wrote papers on the critical mass of social workers necessary to a service economy. His office was just the quiet refuge I needed. Our first interview was so entirely different than I expected that I despaired of his hiring me. We spoke about books, operas, movies, popular culture. Then I told him I didn't want to take dictation. He looked very pained at that declaration. Well, I conceded maybe some dictation. No, he said, he wouldn't want to give dictation to me if I felt strongly about it. In the end, I would be glued to the dictaphone. As it turned out, he was a prolific writer and spoke most of it into a little recorder that he took with him everywhere, in the car, in the early hours of the morning, it didn't matter to him, he was a first class thinker. I was seduced by social theory for hours and hours of dictation. He'd warned me about the isolation. He suggested I take long lunch hours and walk about the campus. He would make me his research assistant and then I could always walk to the library under the pretense of carrying out some research task. By now, I'd earned my bachelors and was taking my first graduate course. It was in postmodernism and deconstruction.

When Professor DiGigante was in, he'd hang his coat, scarf and hat on a coat rack in my outer office. It was the flamboyant act of a flamboyant man. His hat and scarf hung at a rakish angle before my desk – a reminder that he was within and that there was a good chance we'd go to lunch. Those were the best days. The school was near one of the more affluent towns on the Island and when John DiGigante took me to lunch it was often to one of the better restaurants in town. He liked living well, taking his revenge on the academic establishment that had thrown him over by driving a good fast car, drinking twenty-year-old scotch and satisfying a silver palate. We'd have the best conversations over lunch. A few times he took me out to places on the water so that he could inquire about a slip at the marina for his boat.

Ever since I'd gone to work at the university Sam had been making my life hell. Practically every morning he drove me to work we'd argue and I'd get out of the car with him at my back swearing and shouting at me for the entire world to hear. I'd walk upstairs to my office with a sickening feeling in the pit of my stomach. He was wearing me down, undermining what little self-esteem I could muster up to work at something new, something I really wanted to do. What was worse, I felt that I had to hide his abuse, had to put on a face for the world. Then I'd had to endure the dismantling of the department, and, while working for DiGigante was intellectually invigorating, I was, nevertheless, back to being a secretary, a role in which I was profoundly ambivalent. I wasn't making enough money.

I began to have arthritic symptoms, pain from the shoulder to the wrist. The vertebra at the base of my neck was swollen and there was swelling at the inside of one elbow. My doctor suspected from my blood profile that it was rheumatoid arthritis. It was the end of the semester, final time. I was writing a paper for my graduate class and Sam and I were barely speaking to one another. He had all the lights off in the house when I came home and the kitchen would be cold and unfriendly. He was unkempt, he drank during the day and he slept most of the time. I decided to divorce him. My last days in DiGigante's office were spent talking out my marriage with Sam on the phone. He fought hard and I was emotionally exhausted and finally acquiesced. Then one of the writers who'd been fired from the department called and told me about a job she thought would be perfect for me at the university where she was working in the city. I would more than double my salary. I told John DiGigante that I'd never leave him for any reason except money. He understood. Sam went to see a psychiatrist who diagnosed melancholia. I went to work in the city.

111

Tuesday, April 26, 1994

Cher ebon ami,

If I were you, I'd consider this a perfect opportunity to learn what it is to be the object in the "subject-object split." Instead, you choose to further inure the subject. By so doing, you reinforce your original and limited impressions of me. You draw the same conclusions over and over again. You imprison me. I am, of course, always somewhat surprised and charmed by this quality of stubborn insistence on one truth, by your refusal to be swayed even a little by the array of experiences I bring you.

By suggesting I reintegrate myself, you're suggesting a unified approach to life, a certain "oneness" of mind and action that would eliminate or at the very least diminish the complexity and contradictions, the absurd and the ironic of life from which I take some comfort. I don't aspire to unity in thought and deed. As I've often remarked, I've lived on the margin so long, I've come to enjoy it! The sport metaphor of sinking a basket you used was wonderful, but I've never had the opportunity to shoot from center court. It's a man's experience of transcendence. I'm more the strategist, the coach, than I am the star player. My sense of accomplishment doesn't usually reside in the existential act, so much as it does in bringing together disparate parts into odd combinations. The metaphor of weaving would be more appropriate. Still, I know in my bones the transcendent feeling you described. My triumphs, however, when they are of that sort are won, as I told you, as if in a dream, never in the full flush of empowerment. Empowerment comes with the realization of self. In the moment you described I'm separated from self and only my will is operable. I envy you the source of that metaphor, but I would suggest that you're like a horse who must wear blinders in order to win the race. I prefer my peripheral vision.

Soft spring is at my window tonight and the neighbor's kids are playing downstairs in the street. I feel very easy in my skin. I was struck last evening by how hungry for experience some of us are. After I left you, I joined some friends for dinner. One of

112

the guests was an 81-year-old jazz musician, a gallant knight from another day, a substantial man, his hair and skin grizzled now. I call him "Gentleman Jack" because he was such a polished personality when he played the Catskills with Sam years ago. He's a trumpet player, retired from the life and living in his hometown upstate after years of wandering and one-night stands with name performers and nobodies. He listens avidly to the rest of us at the table and drinks in the jokes and stories as if they were life support. At the end of the evening, he confesses that he has nothing to go back to – that nothing is happening in Rome, New York. I much prefer musicians to businessmen. Always have. They seem to wrestle with the same life issues as I do.

My physician says that unless I'm in discomfort, there's no immediate reason to treat my problem. I sometimes wonder how to go about defining pain or discomfort. Since Jane died, I hardly feel hot or cold. I don't know to what extent I would have to be in physical pain before I knew it as discomfort. Certainly, I should never want to be called upon to pronounce someone dead. It would take me a long time to determine death from life.

What a big book you've given me 'bon ami. What a huge task it is! Nevertheless, I have the feeling that you wished in some way to include me--that you wanted me to know something of what you know. How graciously you impose psychology on me, how consistently I resist you.

My dear friend, I'm strangely empty this evening. No recollections rise up from this bruised heart, and I don't want to speak to you in someone else's words. The weather has taken me over and I'm hopelessly nostalgic. Tomorrow is "Secretary's Day" and my boss has invited me to lunch with him and the office manager. These days I vacillate between appreciating the security of my position and what that means in terms of my family and flashes of buried ambition, wishes that surface to be more useful and authentic, to have both responsibility and authority. From moment to moment, I assess my "work" in this fashion. Shall I accept my lot? Is it too late to do anything else? Will I disrupt my family? What is possible?

I have a friend in California who is an actress. She's expressed an interest in excerpting from the letters for a dramatic reading. I'm sending her a copy, but have changed all the names, including my own. My mentor hasn't returned my originals as he promised. I tell myself he's read them and he's intrigued. I tell myself I'm not wasting myself on unrealistic projects and meaningless work. I work and rework the material. I juggle my moods. I keep my promises. I dream of difference. And I am as always,

moi-meme, sain et sauf

Jess

For a long while I'd known that something was growing inside me....

Tuesday, May 3, 1994

Cher ebon ami,

We're like two old worn shoes, you and I. We know each other's soft footfall and distinctive print in the dust. You're beginning to feel like my second skin, mon ami. In these letters, you're the "catcher" and I'm the "sender." What a welcome reversal! What a respite this is for me from being the recipient, the receiver, always acted upon, never acting. I revel in the creation of these letters, in the thought that I'm influencing you, that you read and reread my words. In these pages, I live happy and complete. I believe that writing the letters sustains me, has become my mechanism for coping.

Today I discussed the nature of my work with my boss. I asked to be considered for additional duties. He's set me a task. I'm to write down what I did in the past, what I'm doing now, and what special projects I might do in the future. In essence, he's placed the ball squarely back in my court. Instead of coming to him empty handed, he wants me to come prepared with a well thought out proposal. He won't "make" work for me. He took a solid stand and I admire him. I think I can learn from him.

I asked him about my request a month ago for a salary review. He said he was going to take it up with the human resource consultants he's planning to meet with next week. And since I believe that making someone consciously aware of a situation is often action enough, I'm rather pleased with myself overall.

Today I received in the mail a sheaf of poems from a musician whom I'm very fond of—I may have mentioned him to you recently. His wife died of breast cancer several years ago. I knew her very briefly, but she was a vital force in the lives around her and I can't forget several conversations we had and, in particular, what I saw in her eyes as she came up the front steps when they came for dinner toward the end. I remember waking the next morning in sheer despair. I'd prepared a lavish dinner and she'd hardly been able to eat. She'd sat at the table with such dignity and grace, her beautiful oval face framed by an elegant turban that hid the ravages of chemotherapy. I didn't realize at the time how sick she must have been. After that, they went to ground, drew the cloak of privacy around them until her death. The poems are full of irony and wonder.

Your suggestion that I should write more than the letters lies on the fault line between my private and public life where I continue to brood over it, as well as the question of useful and productive work. Nevertheless, I'm not immune to the greening of my world, to the springtime that's happening around me. I should like to run away. But I can't, of course. And sometimes, just sometimes, I think I've begun to feel slight stirrings of the kind of wisdom that comes with age and a certain kind of resignation.

I think what I've been wrestling with this past week is the notion of compensation. Meaningful work compensates me for a less than perfect personal life. At work, I'm negotiating monetary compensation. Money, I find, if I accept the premise that I deserve it, also has its compensations.

I suppose it's because of the novel I'm reading (I picked it up at a book sale at the Knights of Columbus for ten cents), *A Woman of Property*, by Mabel Seeley (written in 1947!!) that I'm brought to mind of my first marriage. Seeley writes in the frontispiece, "This is a story of hungers which seem to propel much of humanity, and something of humanity must therefore be reflected here." It's the story of a young immigrant girl in a small town in 1889 who aspires to become one of "The Others," to have money and position, to be accepted into that charmed circle she's hungrily and silently watched like a child pressed against the glass of the candy shop. She learns to use manipulation as a strategy to get what she wants. But actually, she's manipulative only within the limits of her circumstances which are defined by the society at large. For women, there are only limited strategies—proscribed scripts. When she's ruined by one young man, she cleverly seduces another into marrying her.

Michael graduated from the university the semester before I became pregnant. He'd already returned to New York when he called me that day to find out whether I'd received the roses he'd sent and I blurted out my secret. He caught the next plane and when he arrived at the campus, we left the campus together for Chicago. He never went back to New York and I never returned to school. A week later, we were married by a judge in chambers and spent our first night as man and wife in a hotel in downtown Chicago. I remember thinking how barbaric a ritual it was—I should have been in the lap of a loving family, surrounded by well wishers and advice givers, and instead here I was in a seedy hotel room with a man who I didn't really love and who'd contracted a venereal disease. I felt not only violated, but also contaminated. I was the thinnest I'd ever been. All my clothes and personal things were still in my dorm room at school. Michael went and packed them up and brought them back to Chicago. I was too ashamed.

For the first few weeks we stayed at my mother's house. I didn't go to my family doctor. My mother sent me to a doctor who'd performed an abortion on her eleven years before. He had a clinic where I went to receive a series of injections to "bring on my period." Every evening I went back to the clinic and the doctor asked me if I'd felt anything. You're a strong woman, he told me in a thick accent. On the third day, I felt the slightest stir of discomfort. Suddenly, I didn't want to lose whatever was growing inside of me. I got in bed and I stayed there.

When Jane was born we were living in a tiny one-bedroom apartment in the treetops. It was on the third floor of a brownstone and it had a lovely sun porch that overlooked the tops of stately Chicago elms. I'd planned to make the sunroom the baby's room and I hung diaphanous pink draperies all across the porch windows. She was a colicky baby—I was a nervous mother. I'd requested they give me a shot to dry up my milk (I couldn't forgive my body for betraying me so) and so I was laid up in bed with ice packs on my distended breasts and between my legs where I'd torn before they could do an episiotomy. They'd sewed me up with heavy black thread (knitting yarn, my family doctor called it). I had my first depressive break.

Seventeen months later, Cara was born. In the spring. In the eighth month of my pregnancy, federal agents arrested Michael at the ticket counter of the airlines where he worked. He'd embezzled money. We'd moved by then to a larger apartment on the first floor of an apartment building that faced a little pocket park.

When I brought Cara home from the hospital, Michael was out of jail and had gone to court and made restitution (my mother went with him, his family never came). The lawyer, who owed my family a favor, saw to it that he had no record. But he was out of a job and my brother was sleeping on the living room couch, also unemployed. I was 22 years old. I had two babies and a compulsive gambler for a husband and my brother, whose bleached hair hung to his shoulders, wore an earring in one ear and came home bloodied one night. Some boys had beaten him up in the pocket park across the way.

The night is very still outside my window. I marvel at the fortitude of that girl so many years ago. But she was wholly ferocious and anger fueled her hunger, while anger only eats at my soul and lays naked my fears.

117

I feel tonight as if I'm your only patient, mon ami. Jusqu'a Lundi,

Moi-meme, sain et sauf

Jess

Wednesday evening, May 11, 1994

Cher ebon ami,

There's much for me to contemplate from our last session. When I asked if I could come to you every other week instead of on a weekly basis, the request and your immediate acquiescence produced a good many doubts and fears in me. Actually I was operating on two different levels. On the one hand, according to my external and immediate situation, I'll gain from seeing you less; on the other, according to my inner wants and needs, I'll probably lose.

But you, you're so unresisting, so completely generous and accommodating and so lacking in motive that you can only benefit. It's evident that you don't want to cause any more anxiety than I'm already dealing with in my everyday life. I should've much preferred, however, if you'd suggested I see you less often as a measure of my success in therapy. You spoke of a young woman as one of your "successes." Am I one of your successes?

I can't help thinking that my financial difficulties—paying for Mimi's therapy and our losing our tenant are what make it possible for me to withdraw from you and hold back ever so slightly at a particularly uncomfortable point in our relationship. Have I come to the point where acceptance and resignation should supplant action and argument? You've thrown me some left field curves lately. Am I so inured to loss that I can't feel emotion unless it's the emotion of grief and deprivation? Was it a test on my part? Did I really want you to say, "absolutely not,

118

Tess, you're finally becoming visible and you want to fade back into the background, hide behind the needs of your family. I won't allow it. You must put yourself and your own needs first. I insist you come to see me every week. Just when we're making progress, you disrupt the therapy." Of course, I'm so used to the rhythm of disruption—it's the natural music of my life. And then, your self-interest in insisting I come would have proved I was important, even if only as a paying customer.

It's a busy time at work—I have a Board meeting coming up and I'm responsible for the preparation of a docket for the meeting. The boss is giving me more authority. I'm doing more phone work, coordinating more meetings, following up with the staff more. Having real work to do invigorates me. The other day he came back from one of our big corporate members with a comprehensive outline for compensation. A new employee policy manual should be in place by the fall. I have hopes that it will be a better place to work. I've also worked on updating my resume. A friend has begun networking with a prominent foundation which she feels I might be interested in working for—just as nothing stays good forever, nothing stays bad forever either, eh my dear friend? Even the suggestion of movement makes me feel as if I'm not stagnating, standing still as time moves forward.

You said I had a fertile imagination. What, I wonder, did you mean by that. A lively mind can break itself on the rocks of illusion and deception, you know. Can it be that only a year ago, I was at Mercy, ravaged by depression? Has it been a whole year that I've been coming to see you 'bon ami? Perhaps it's time for a progress report.

In many ways, I feel I've managed to triumph over this season's power to bruise my heart. Sam is active and his spirits are good. Mimi's made it to the end of the semester with a B+ average and the summer lays before me, a favorite time to do favorite things, read, write and think thoughts, lazy and slow. I'll miss you this Monday, my good doctor. Thank you for responding so quickly to my phone request for a prescription and a bill. En ensemble encore un fois 23 May!

Moi-meme, sain et sauf

Jess

Tuesday, May 17, 1994

Cher ebon ami,

In our last several sessions, you gave me some "absolutes" to
think about and I've been thinking long and hard ever since. One
was about my job. You favor my moving on from this place
where I make little use of my talents and where I'm bound by the
constraints of an office "caste" system that's immutable. In other
words, it's fairly clear I'm going nowhere. You haven't voiced
your feelings until now because you recognize that there are
always ramifications to these kind of decisions and because in
your experience, people proceed with life changes like this at
their own rate and pace. Of course, you're right, but whether I
acted on it or not, I still would have liked to have known what
you thought. The effect of your not being completely candid
with me has been to prolong the conflict about my job. You
underestimate your influence with me and how much I need your
help to establish realistic boundaries. Besides, you're much
more hardheaded than I am; I need that perspective. Otherwise I
struggle continually with what I must accept and what I can
change.

Of course, I realize what a struggle it must be not to make
moral judgments about what I tell you, to maintain a position of
neutrality and fairness, but sometimes it feels as if you're
indifferent, holding back the most precious thing, your subjective
feelings. This diffident attitude impedes the progress we can
make together.

During our last session, pressed perhaps by the prospect of
my seeing you less, you provided me some hard facts. You told
me you thought Sam's impotence was directly related to his
diabetes, that it was damage to blood vessels and nerve endings
— that, in fact, although he may occasionally get a low blood

120

sugar reading, his diabetes will progress in an "inexorable" way. Somehow, it was good to have this so clearly stated. Any doubts or illusions that I may have harbored, any expectations for a return to what was "normal" for us were immediately laid to rest. You killed my hopes, but you gave me something more valuable--you gave me choices. I could say "knowing this, what are my options, how shall I proceed?" And for me, knowing is always much, much better than not knowing.

You asked about my physical condition. Sometimes I almost forget I have a real physical body, I live in my mind so much of the time. One of the most therapeutic parts of lovemaking is that I become aware of my body as my partner reflects it. So it was very good for you to "concretize" my recent experience in discovering something growing inside me, something superfluous and unattractive that came with age and change. You explored with me some of the feelings I might have about having my uterus removed—feelings of loss and castration, of diminished sexual capacity. We discussed anatomy (about which I'm not very knowledgeable) and the source and enhancement of female orgasm (about which I know something). I would very much regret losing ecstasy as I've known it all these years, but basically I believe that removing these growths might very well be an experience of renewal for me.

Oh, how I've missed you this week, 'bon ami--and how many ways I've tried to console myself. Yesterday, at lunchtime, I took a long walk and bought myself some pretty things. Last night, when I would have normally come to see you, I gave up all my ordinary tasks and sat in front of the TV, polishing my nails and eating a rich dessert. I contemplated getting "the works" at the beauty shop and I even scraped together the money to finally replace my reading glasses. I told myself that this week I'd be able to help Mimi with her medical bills. But for all the little charms and tricks I played on myself, I still felt deprived of not being able to see you. Why, I asked myself, had I made you the reader of these letters? Why had it become so necessary that I share my inner thoughts, indeed, my inner life with you and you alone? What special bond was there between us? And always, I returned to one of our earliest sessions and to the quality of "boy" I saw in you--earnest, sincere, imploring me to only not hold back, joyful and ebullient, somewhat irreverent and inquisitive. But you've managed to hold onto these qualities, to remain untouched by cynicism. You haven't fallen. And I, I've lost my girlhood—bright, shining time of lightness and safe places and innocent play. Still I have the feeling that somehow our childhoods touched—that we were connected by unspoken dreams, a world without words.

I've been thinking this week about my mother's last husband. He also had a boyish quality about him and, I suppose, that's why he comes to mind. My mother's marriage to the man whose baggage I'd unceremoniously discovered one day in the middle of the living room, was, by the time I had Jane, just as unceremoniously unraveling. Oh, they still lived together, but they rarely spoke to each other and they had divided the refrigerator and each shopped with their own cart at the supermarket. Theirs was a pitched battle in the kitchen and the bedroom. My mother told me that he continued to come across the bed and have sex when the mood took him, but that it was against her will. Marital rape.

As for my relationship with him, whenever I brought Jane for a visit to Grandma's house, he tended to ascribe all sorts of terrible acts to her. "She ate my laundry ticket," he'd say or some other equally off putting remark. But I owed him something for having come to my rescue one night years before, when my mother was attacking me in a drunken rage. She wanted me to throw him out because he'd taken her by the shoulders and shaken her. He intervened and for that I felt grateful to him. He'd stood up for me that night against what seemed like a formidable foe bent on crushing me. I'd never known a man to take my part before. So I stayed my distance during those last horrible days of their ill fated marriage.

My mother, however, always the realist, had wasted no time in finding someone new. Her sister's husband, who owned an auto repair shop, introduced her to this auto parts salesman. He was a widower, a tall, nattily dressed gentlemen of Swedish and Norwegian descent. He was quiet and decent. So decent that later, after my mother married him, he admitted after having a little too much to drink that he felt guilty for having dated her when she was still married to someone else. They were to remain married for the next twenty years.

I never really knew how to read him. At first, I thought because he was quiet that he was angry with me, but actually, I think he was quite fond of me. One of his sons, standing in the cemetery after his funeral, said that I'd come into his life at the right time. He had no daughters. I never felt that he judged me. And one sunny summer day, standing by the back door of their house, with the cats playing in my mother's flower garden, and the kids tumbling all over the lawn, he asked me to bring him a drink from the house. "A good daughter would get it for me," he said. And thrilled at the prospect of being a "good daughter," I ran to serve him.

When Sam and I were married, he came to New York to our apartment. He sat down at Sam's big Steinway piano and said, "You know, I can play the piano too!" And even though it wasn't his religion, he wore a yarmulke out of respect for our traditions and walked me down the aisle and gave me to Sam in a Jewish ceremony that he couldn't possibly have understood. Then there was the time he came to rescue me and the girls during a tornado when we were stranded in a storefront beauty shop. A huge tree was torn up in front of the building where they lived, but he got in his car and just drove over and picked us up and brought us home as if it all was an everyday event. Another time he walked to the bus stop in a snow storm to carry my girls off the bus in two feet of snow, with me trailing thankfully behind him. He was a craftsman who admired anything that was well made and he was sensitive to beauty. Once he drove me past a hospital just to show me a sculpture made of car fenders mounted on the front of the building. He thought it was beautiful.

The only time I ever drove a car was with him on country roads in Wisconsin. I drove up and down rolling hills, backed into dirt roads and finally turned the car towards home. He let me drive it all the way into their driveway. I managed so well that as he was getting out of the car he said, "That was pretty

123

good. But you've driven before, haven't you?" And when I said no, I'd never driven before, that that was my first time, he said, "Well, I think I need a drink" and walked into the house.

He went fishing with Sam and played solitaire with the girls and every night, before dinner, up in Wisconsin, he'd make him and me a perfect martini. The best in three states, I'd tell him. And my mother hated it. He was a gracious host, good-natured with the townspeople, who all loved him. And as affable and outgoing as he was, she was closed up and mean. Every year, when we came to visit, he'd wait until he got me alone and he'd say, "Well, it's been pretty hard with your mother this year." And then, one year he got the call that his oldest boy, who'd had a history of mental problems and who'd terrified his own family for years, had gone down to the Chicago lakefront on Christmas day and put a bullet in his head. Not long after that, he argued with my mother and ran away from her for three days. He came home with a bleeding ulcer. Then bladder cancer. Finally, they moved back down to Chicago to be near the doctors and the hospital. The cancer spread. At the last, it went to the brain. I had one day with him during that time. One day when my mother didn't scold him or correct him, one day when he spoke to me from his diseased brain and his great heart.

When he died, I was back in school earning my bachelor's degree. It was 1988, three years after Jane's death. It was during finals and I got word that he was gone. My "study buddy" was a man in his 70s, a wonderful man, who helped me to study for my finals when no one else would or could. I remember when I took the last final before leaving for Chicago, I felt like I was writing in great big, huge letters, like a child, but when I got that paper back weeks later, I'd written in a normal hand.

My mother and my brother turned his funeral into a sham, but that's another story for another evening, dear friend. I miss you.

Moi-meme, sain et sauf

Jess

Wednesday, May 24, 1994

Cher ebon ami,

I believe we come to a heightened consciousness of ourselves slowly, as if we're rising to the surface from the depths of an ocean. Something like Emerson's spiralling transcendence. And we take depth soundings at certain levels. Part of this rise is because of a certain permeability we have and part because of the slow float of desire. Part is our will and how we adapt to the various situations and exigencies of life. Only occasionally there are moments of absolute clarity, an epiphany.

And so, in a way, we live many lives in the wake of our evolving consciousness. Lately I have been thinking about who I was when I was young. In contrast to my usual vagueness, I had an energy—call it drive or perhaps it was my will — that neither dissembled nor digressed. I was purposeful and I operated almost always from instinct without worrying whether I was right or wrong. I had a past that I didn't even attempt to decode and a seemingly infinite future. Time was something I could shape and structure in the simple schedules of my children's needs. While I was passionate, I was sexually unaware. I had a certain kind of strength that comes when we act out what we think of as a natural and appropriate destiny. I was sure of myself and unconcerned about everything else around me. And that's the point. I was a sort of amoral young savage with little actual identity--that would come slowly and painfully much, much later and not without its own particular crises. I had a lot of blind drive and certainty based on little else than my own limited insights and experiences. Gutsy. Sometimes it frightens me to think that something so important as a child's formative years depended on that narrow perspective. But then I was free to act and innocent of the ramifications. Was I an independent woman? No. Am I now? Yes, I am.

You know one of the side affects of this therapy with you is that I've become far more articulate in ordinary conversations than I ever was before. I know that I'm less repressed, more

125

myself, when my vocabulary comes to the fore the way it has in recent days. I think it's a good sign that we're aware of the language we use with each other. I prize a new word, one that I've never heard before. Your word "tergiversation" delighted me. However, in my dictionary the first definition of tergiversate is "to desert a cause" and the second is "to be clever or tricky in avoiding responsibility"!

One of my first recollections from childhood has to do with the sound of words. Our first home was an apartment house on the corner of Parker and Long directly across from the Schubert Elementary school, a very grand looking edifice of red brick and white granite. It was during the war and my mother worked nights in a munitions factory. She made shell casings for bombs, threaded the metal on a machine. She slept during the day and I played in her bedroom at the window to be close to her. The windows in the apartment faced the front of the building and I remember that I had one of my brother's trucks that I ran back and forth across the sill. "And the pumpernickel truck is going to the factory to pick up the pumpernickel bread and deliver the pumpernickel bread to all the people," I would say over and over sotto voce, so as not to wake my mother. I'd discovered the word pumpernickel and I played with it, rolling the syllables over my tongue, puffing the "puh" sound, coming down hard on the "n." It was such a satisfying word. It was all I had to play with and it was more than enough. Words have always been my friends. Still, it occurs to me that we engaged in very little talk, conversation or wordplay at home. It's from all the reading I've done that I gleaned my vocabulary. So that language used as part of social behavior is a good measure of my mental wellbeing, since it's always been a part of my solitude. Years ago, I admitted in group therapy that one of my greatest fears was having to attend "ladies luncheons." I suppose I feared being inarticulate. Making small talk -- but that's another story -- I wasn't made to make small talk, I think you'll readily agree.

I'm less anxious knowing that I will see you at the appointed hour.

Jusqu'a Lundi, I'm still

Moi-meme, sain et sauf

Jess

Tuesday evening, May 31, 1994

Cher ebon ami,

Let's talk about female sexuality, human sexuality and the specifics of my situation without assigning a gender to any particular act of will or sexual practice, shall we? Let's talk about the components of seduction, ardor, desire, common to both partners. Let's allow for my subjectivity in our discussions, along with yours and Sam's. And most importantly, let's not buy into silly sexual myths about two kinds of orgasm, one deeper and more preferable than the other. It's a worn-out tale perpetrated on women to keep them perpetually in chains.

Despite the fact that I was thrown into a rage by your fascination with Sam's overwhelming need to possess me, and despite Sam's clarifying his statement (what he really meant was that he wanted control over his own body), our frank and open discussion last night did serve to clarify some of the issues I presently face in my relationship with him, indeed I suspect that underlie heterosexual relationships in general.

Ever mindful that it's a phallogocentric world we live in, but that within that context I can either withhold or allow access to my body, at what point then does my ardor, arousal and readiness enter the picture? What about sexual overtures that I might make? Is a woman only in a position to say yea or nay? Granted that with my consent and by my own free will I surrender under particular circumstances (ardor and readiness) to penetration by a penis, in actuality, it's not the penis that's important to me. It's the erection of his penis that's important to me since, I believe, I've been instrumental in creating that erection.

However, in our discussion, we (you and I), were guilty of construing this singular act of entrance or penetration by my partner as the entire sexual act. We have, in our haste to solve one area of dysfunction ignored the myriad intricate mutual signals, exquisite timing, and elegant rhythms that exist between a man and a woman before, during and after sex. Your capsule description of our lovemaking was patently mundane and unsophisticated, because it captured only the most gross body movements and motor skills of foreplay necessary for access to and penetration of a woman's body—she invites, he presses the usual buttons and voila, instant access. You assumed that an almost automatic response to penetration was orgasm. I'm left with the most mundane of master/slave, dominant/submissive scenarios.

So let me begin. The correspondent response to male penetration is a welcoming engulfment, envelopment, which is the physical act of surrounding and grasping vaginally the other. When we speak about the stroke of an erect penis, aren't we also speaking about the correspondent thrust of a woman's hips and pelvis reaching upward, rocking toward the desired other, affirming and reaffirming her assent and rising passion?

Sexual intercourse isn't merely a one-sided seduction that disguises a struggle for control—good sex involves giving up control, as a matter of fact. Nor is it a frivolous occupation to be entered into lightly and accomplished with toys in order to produce ever-increasing sensation and reaction. That's exploitation and objectification whether performed on oneself or on another.

When we speak of sexuality, we speak of an important and ongoing part of shared human experience, perhaps, the most important part of human experience, certainly one of the most primal of human needs. One is sexually pleasured in a number of ways. To ascribe all the intricate and complex nuances of my sexuality to gratification by male penetration and frequent orgasm is to do an extreme injustice to my capacity to go beyond the limits of love as I perceive them. For me sexual love is not about self-love or object-love. I'm indignant that you and Sam would suggest that I lovingly respond to a lifeless and absurd object fashioned after a penis. It's idol worship of the worst kind, a tyranny of the phallus that you're suggesting. You conflate two separate issues, pleasure and sensation; you assign me a limited, if not totally empty role as a mere reflection of male potency. You would make me into a caricature of myself. For I'm enamored of sexual surrender, but not for any of the reasons you might surmise. I find it inevitably empowering. To give in is not necessarily to give up. And I'm very virile and sexually potent in my own right, my friend. I enjoy the rhythms of straightforward fucking, the athleticism of it, being able to measure my own stamina and endurance against that of another, being able to give pleasure as well as receive it.

Over and above the particulars I've spoken about, there's the question of how I perceive my sexuality as an ongoing and changing element of my life. Had you considered this, you would have seen how impossible it is for me to accept simplistic remedies and how important it is that I don't feel my sexuality falling into degeneracy.

Well, sex is a fruitful subject and I'm very tempted to try for an essay since you fellows have gotten me in a "full court press" to borrow a metaphor from basketball! But I'm preoccupied with work. Tomorrow is the Board of Directors meeting and I've been working away at planning and coordinating it these last several weeks. But let me close with a quote from a very fine and thoughtful book written by one of my professors at CUNY, Roslyn Bologh. Her book is called *Love or Greatness* and it's an analysis of the philosophy of Max Weber. In a chapter titled, "Erotic Love as Coercion," Bologh writes:

> Is desire inherently a coercive element in a relationship...If male dominance is an essential feature of masculinity as defined by our culture, then self-consciousness of masculinity, a self-conscious critique of masculinity as male dominance, should make it theoretically possible to transform male identity and eliminate the coercion deriving from male privilege. But if coercion is inherent in the expression of desire itself, the imposition of one's will on another, then the

problem is not even theoretically resolvable except through a self-disciplined renunciation of erotic love, a learning to discipline sexual desire as opposed to elevating it into erotic love.

Bologh has set the problem here. She concludes:

"What is between us makes a difference to each of us; that is, it links us and differentiates us from each other. We learn from what is between us, who we are: how we are similar, how we differ. What is between us brings us together, sifts us, mingles us, but also stays between us revealing our essential separateness and difference. What is between us is not simply our bodies as it is in narrow patriarchal notions of eros."

Good stuff, eh? Suffice to say Sam and I continue to talk about "what is between us" as do you and I. Jusqu'a Lundi, I remain,

Moi-meme, sain et sauf

Jess

June 7, 1994

Dear friend,

I feel as if I'm guarding my daughter Mimi with my life these days. It's an emotionally exhausting task, as you must know. But it helps a great deal to know that you're poised and ready if I need you. How foolish I feel about hesitating to call on you during this crisis. Certainly it's no time to observe all the niceties and courtesies of a formal relationship, when my daughter's experiencing a depressive break. You were right to ask why I didn't call you. Just for that moment, I thought I'd failed in a task you set. I'm so used to meeting every need and requirement of others that I forgot I can call you if I need you, forgot that you're willing to help me, that part of our unspoken contract is that you'll freely share the benefit of your knowledge. There's something to be learned about me from this, however. I couldn't bear it if you refused me.

It's difficult to tell when Mimi will "bottom out" in her capacity to inflict self-punishment and it frightens me. At the same time, it's painful to listen to the extent of her anguish and grief. She mourns the ideal from which she's fallen, she fears the continuing fall. World without end of pain and anger, shame and guilt. It is my difficult work to bear witness to my daughter's sorrows. Every night I fall onto my bed, tired and wordless to express the penumbra of feelings that fall on me like a pack of hungry wolves, savaging me.

When we spoke in front of your house about anger and I told you that my feeling of righteous indignation had a certain cleansing effect on me right now, now when I'm confronted by my daughter's undifferentiated rage, a rage that's so all consuming that she must inevitably turn it upon herself, I think I was letting you know that indignation is one of my most reliable coping mechanisms. It preserves an intact ego. It's a way to avoid the kind of "splitting" off you referred to when you were talking about Mimi's impulsive behavior and tendency toward self-abuse. I've learned to fight the subject-object split in this manner. You know, if a man sits on a chair and the chair leg breaks and he's spilled unceremoniously on the floor, he assumes there's something wrong with the chair. If a woman has the same experience, she assumes that either she sat on the chair the wrong way or she weighs too much! Either way she blames herself, he blames the object. To cultivate a healthy indignation is to blame the object for not supporting the subject. I wish I saw more of this in Mimi.

When she was a little girl, she had a habit of reifying inanimate objects. "Hello, my sunshine" she would say, "you've come to play with me." And she had a blanket, a "softy blanky" that was a great source of comfort. At one point I tried to hide it on her, it was in rags, but she found it in my closet and immediately took it up as if it were a long lost friend, crowing and crooning to it.

I'm in touch with her therapist and she's conferred with the prescribing psychiatrist at Stony Brook. Mimi is going to call tomorrow and make an appointment for a psychiatric evaluation. In the meantime, they've temporarily raised the dosage to 150 mgs. and providing the evaluation supports it, they want to place her on an anti-anxiety drug. Her therapist has stipulated that I dispense the drug to Mimi. Both recommend that she not be left alone for any amount of time (but my sense of the thing told me this already) and that if I'm alarmed or she takes another sudden dip, that I act on my judgment and use the plan you and I discussed.

Despite my immediate pressures and worries, I have to tell you that I was secretly happy that you were worried about me the other evening when I was late for our session. It's rare that anyone is worried about me without being worried about themselves. I savored your stern look and the gentle chiding you gave me.

'Bon ami, I'm so sleepy these past few days. I could literally fall asleep on my feet. It's the intensity of my situation. I've begun to have menopausal flashes and associated symptoms, as well. I'm determined not to give in to any of it. I've thought of you often this week. You're right. If I come out of this simply myself I'll consider ours a fortuitous relationship. Please forgive the brevity of this letter--I'm almost wholly taken up with my daughter's cares.

Jusqu'a Lundi, I'm

Moi-meme, sain et sauf

Jess

Tuesday evening, June 14, 1994

Cher ebon ami,

Through all of this I have my sanity. I have your encouragement. I have the help of friends. And so I continue.

As I told you at our last visit, it's very hard to watch Mimi in this full-blown depression, to recognize myself and many of the others from Mercy in my daughter's despair and mortification. But I'm bound to her by the strongest of bonds – my daughter, myself – and I can't look away. I study her, the light and shadow on the planes of her face, the unblinking eyes, and the slack lips, for a sign of the person she was only a week ago. But that person isn't this tormented girl I see before me. Will she ever come back?

Coming home on the train this evening, I fell into a light sleep. I woke at midpoint—Jamaica, and for that moment I felt lighthearted and renewed. Our talks this past year have been of enormous help to me lately. More than you would ever suppose.

Well, the kitten is a fait accomplit. Sam understands that Mim needs to give herself to some living thing right now. And all I can think of is this poem by Gerard Manley Hopkins that begins "Margaret are you grieving over goldengrove unleaving." My girl has traversed boundaries I never would have. She looks into an abyss only she can see. She has a hasty heart. She speaks in slurred whispered tones to me of her pain. I'm her father confessor and her mother superior, poor soul.

I imagined last week when I couldn't reach you that you'd fled before my troubles, fled the burden of my needs. Where once I feared my life to be too sordid for your confidence, now I fear you've broken all covenants with me. The events of my life have become like an anvil and I am being beaten into pure steel and you, you've flown up like a shower of sparks from the force of it. And still, I continue.

There was a beautiful sky this evening and I'm struck by how much we miss of the beauty this world has to offer when we are low with depression. I sleep these evenings, my friend. And without calling the genie out of the bottle. But I must admit I

133

summon your strength and innocence, your very darkness to me as I fall asleep.

I'm very concerned about keeping a viable appointment time with you. You know, I've planned to weekend in the country this summer. Am I going to have to choose?

Words hold little solace for me tonight. I'm a creature of the senses these past few days. I must hear you, see you, speak with you to reassure me that you're actually there, my kindly interrogator. Thank God for friendship.

Jess

Monday evening, June 20, 1994

Cher ebon ami,

During this tumultuous time, when practically every word and action that arises from the bond between my daughter and myself wounds me to the quick one way or another, I'm strangely self-possessed. I'm capable of continuing on my own path, making personal decisions and even being distracted by interest and desire. Perhaps this is a sign of the inevitable onset of adulthood. Perhaps. Or is it a sign that I'm unwilling to go over the precipice with her, that not only are we not synchronized in this fashion, but that I'm distinctly less willing than she to give up everything for oblivion. I no longer believe that meaning resides in the Other. Sam is no longer the center of my life. Psychic pain doesn't diminish me the way it used to do. I've been thinking about coercion and the exercise of free will. About how we give power back to my daughter who has contrived to surrender it so completely.

The newest addition to our family, a six week-old kitten we call Inky continues to do his work -- bring my daughter out of herself. If he only knew how important he is to our household, how much of our mutual wellbeing is owed to his fragile little shape, his innocent, quizzical gaze, his ersatz bravado, leaping out at our feet from corners, sitting neatly in a tiny pose, gravely attentive to our human goings ons!

Listen to this from a novella called *Immaculate Man* written by Mary Gordon and included in a recent book called *The Rest of Life*:

> When a man invents a woman, he invents emptiness. Some place to disappear inside. He hollows out, he scoops out what's already there; the wet seeds of a melon. He discards, he darkens, he obscures. For us, it's much more difficult. What must we invent? From nothing, from a whole cloth? A fortress, a stone monument, a face to fill the gap, Virgil, Orpheus, a steering wheel, an engine. A solidity. That's why Psyche couldn't stand it there with Eros: the invention in the dark. A man might have enjoyed it. We do not enjoy the dark. We aren't after emptiness. Why would we be housing our own emptiness, or knowing that at any time someone may be getting ready to empty us, or getting ready for the emptiness, to fill or deny it, to inhabit it or wall it off.

Pretty good stuff, eh?

Mimi is much, much better – it's remarkable the resilience of the young. She's come back like a rubber band rebounding into shape. By the way, I did look up "splitting" in the book you lent me – it aptly describes one of the problems she'll have to work through in the coming months (there are many, she is a tissue of confusions and misperceptions, competing values and massive frustrations). We're such fragile creatures after all. And it's an age of anxiety. I can only rely on intuition. Hers is a huge protest.

To have two completely different situations taking place in the family at once, the jubilation we feel over Cara's having landed an internship in the Mayor's Office, and the discouragement and near despair of Mimi's recent depressive episode, is unfamiliar territory for me. I'm afraid I've considered us a sort of monolithic suffering unit up until now. Events have decentered my world, you might say.

In retrospect, I'm rather proud of how I handled myself at our last meeting. I wish there were something aesthetically pleasing to give you in this letter, my friend. The world isn't looking too beautiful to me these days. See you on Saturday at the new time -- it strikes me that change may be healthy, but not much fun.

I am, somewhat precariously and with many little aftershocks,

Moi-meme, sain et sauf

Jess

We had decided to meet on Saturdays and he was working toward meeting on an "as needed" basis. Something had changed, the slightest shift had occurred in our relationship. I thought that maybe he was being reviewed at the hospital. He asked what I intended to do with the letters. He knew by this time that I'd kept copies of all the letters and that I thought they might make a book. But he was particularly interested in who would edit the letters. And he seemed to be slightly distracted during our sessions, as if he was silently counting or taking inventory. But I was so caught up in my own chain of events, I put any thoughts about his discomfort out of my mind.

Monday, June 27, 1994

Cher ebon ami,

I have precious little solitude these days in which to speculate or reminisce -- the demands of my family and certain social obligations preclude it. For me, it's risky business to be so active a participant in my own life. Of course, it's been heartening to watch my daughter spring back from the depths of depression. So many positive things go into the recovery of a

136

personality – I hadn't realized. She's actually every bit the young woman I would like her to be -- a strong, independent thinker, a good judge of people, sensitive and intuitive, and guided by an inner logic, a sort of internal gyroscope that I've always lacked. She gets it from her father, I think. She suffers, however, from a great many confusions, misperceptions and misplaced values. I have to rely on the strength of the bond between us and the therapeutic process to reawaken her basic integrity.

Mostly these days, it's a matter of wisely handling my resources. I've never thought of it that way, perhaps because I've never felt I had much in the way of "resources" and I mean both inner resources like courage, hope, faith, ingenuity and inspiration, as well as tangible external resources like money, time and people that I can count on.

The hardest part of "living" like this is not being able to work on the letters and other writings, since this kind of living doesn't seem to allow for reading and writing. You mentioned at our last session that I'd broken out of what you called my "character shell." It seems to me that the contradictory drives to immerse myself in something greater and for autonomy, are simultaneously at work in my life. And certain needs and desires have been temporarily and necessarily repressed during this time. Crisis seems to act on me like an appetite suppressant. I have craved music however. But it must be music without words. I've been listening to classical music again during my commute, hoping, I suppose, that it will provide me a certain regulation of emotions, yes even forgetfulness, a few peaceful moments of respite from my life's story. That's what's happening right now. I'm writing my life by living it and so I'm unable to historicize it in my usual way, with you, 'bon ami.

The role I play these days is not particularly feminine -- my daughter's well being is too important to me for me to concern myself with social constructions. Nevertheless, she refuses to allow me to provide her what she believes her father should rightfully provide—financial support and provenance or definition. It's ironic, isn't it, that she insists upon these artificial

divisions—like insisting that I wear pink and he wear blue—
even now when she's so needy.

Sam has let down under the strain of recent events and we
had a terrible argument last night. Actually it's never an
argument, because he raises his voice and puts a stop to all
possible conversation. He knows we will all be changed from
this crisis and by the possibility of my getting a raise in salary
and he hates when things change. He can't adapt, indeed, he
can't even think an issue through. He's like an open wound.
And he despairs...

Escape. I take the girls and go tomorrow evening. We'll fly
to Chicago and visit with old friends, attend a family wedding
and have some time together, just the three of us. It reminds me
of that quote from Alfred Kazin, "in the midst of death we are in
life -and itching to get away for the weekend."

Your thoughts on memory and forgetfulness made me think
of Alfred, Lord Tennyson's poem, *The Lotos-Eaters*. Of course,
to eat the lotos is to lose one's will. I'll miss you this week, mon
medecin bon. But I always have the best of what we are with
me.

Moi-meme, sain et sauf

Jess

Wednesday evening, July 6, 1994

Cher ebon ami,

Where to start? I feel as if I've been away for weeks and it's
only been a few days in Chicago. But these few days held so
much emotion and deep associations that I could have been
living a lifetime. For awhile, I forgot even you.

On my return, there was a message on the answering
machine from my mother. She must have known that my
nephew was getting married and that we were in Chicago for the
wedding. This is not the first time that she's tried to contact me

after I've been with our relatives. But the shocking part was that I didn't recognize the voice on the machine -- not even the cadences, the timbre or the speech patterns. I knew it was her from the message, but I didn't recognize the voice. She said that it was an emergency, otherwise she wouldn't be calling. She said her brother was dying and that she wanted the address at Brandeis University so that when he died, she could send a check to my daughter Jane's scholarship fund. She said I could call her back and she left her number. Then she thanked us very formally and hung up.

It took me a while to work out what I was feeling besides for the general deflation such news brings when I've just come from a joyous event. At first I was caught up in the news that my uncle was dying. I felt a certain responsibility to articulate sympathy and grief. But then, I went over her initial statement "This is an emergency, otherwise I would never call." And I found it simply wasn't true. It may be an emergency for her. I seriously doubt that it is since her sister had piteously pleaded with her from her deathbed to come and she'd steadfastly refused. Nevertheless it wasn't an emergency for me. I've known for years that my uncle Ted's health was failing, that he had heart problems and that he was getting on in years. I've always had supreme faith in my aunt Jean's judgment and so I knew that if it was necessary for me to know his condition, or indeed, even about his death, my aunt would either write or call me. I also knew that I wasn't prepared to take any extreme measures in the event of his death –for instance, I wouldn't travel to Chicago for his funeral.

My mother was perfectly capable, certainly even more so with the aid of my brother and his wife who are close to her, of obtaining the information she was ostensibly seeking from another source. She didn't need to speak to me. She wanted to speak to me. And it was as much to upset my happiness as it was to assuage her guilty feelings, alienation and despair. Once I was able to recognize her pattern, despite being unable to recognize her voice, I could deal with it. I let it slip away from me. I took up my everyday life where I'd left it.

Sam's gone up to the mountains to work at one of the hotels for the summer. I believe the separation will be good for us both. Mimi grows stronger and better by the day. I'm reassured by demonstrations of her judgment and of her will. Instinctual drives are as important as reason, I think. I've learned some things from spending the past several days in close quarters with both my daughters. I never dreamed how difficult it might be to separate from someone like me—how hard it's been for my girls to individually develop in their own path. They tell me they've often been overwhelmed by my introspection and analytic approach to life, that at times they had to really struggle not to be consumed by me.

'Bon ami, it's terribly warm this evening up here in my study and I grow increasingly impatient to see you in the flesh. It seems our last session was in another life. Lassitude overtakes me. Just know that I'm well and full of plans for the next weeks and months. But I'll tell you all about it when I see you. I hope your little family is having a pleasant summer.

Moi-meme, sain et sauf

Jess

Monday evening, July 11, 1994

Cher ebon ami,

How good it is to be back in the same world with you! To reestablish a frame of reference for the events that transpire in my everyday life. It did seem as if I'd been away for ages, so much to process. I'm afraid I seemed a little garbled and ran on as I have a tendency to do. But there was so much to tell. Mainly about the different relationships. It amazes me how families reconstitute themselves in such fascinating permutations and alliances. Actually I find it fascinating and a little bit frightening. There sometimes seems to be no end to it (I suppose I'm really afraid that there is no beginning to it!)

I'm beginning to like our Saturday morning sessions -- sometimes you still look blurred and thick with sleep like a little boy when I come in. And I like to see you in your weekend clothes--it makes me glad I've decided to remain a part of your private practice (your dedication to your work at the hospital makes me uneasy about my own relation to community, I'm afraid). Forgive me these small indulgences, 'bon ami. Whenever I go away, I find myself filled with true affection for the men in my life.

I spent last Saturday afternoon with Lenny, my business partner. In the dark coolness of his apartment, in the middle of editing the letters on his computer, I fell sound asleep on his living room couch for two hours! Lenny's a big gentle giant of a man -- he calls himself a "misplaced academic." He's the possessor of a wealth of information about a great many subjects. He loves his computer and he used to love chess, but I don't know if he does anymore. Perhaps it's too adversarial for him these days. But he continues to socialize with his friends from the chess club. He has soft hands and soft lips and an absolute tolerance for you if you're his friend. I must have needed to revisit the shelter of his place after all the travel and the jumble of emotions I'd been through.

Oh, what a good book I've stumbled upon during a serendipitous search of the library shelves, mon ami. It's called *Voice Lessons: On Becoming a (Woman) Writer* and it's written by an extraordinary woman, Nancy Mairs. I call her extraordinary because she's that rare breed of feminist who has escaped the pitfalls and pratfalls of academia and headed out into what she refers to as "the wild zone." "The wild zone," she writes, "is the abode of female spirituality." It's almost too painful to read this book since it's as if she lives under my skin—that's how closely I can identify with what she writes. On writing essays:

> I want a prose that is allusive and translucent, that eases you into me and embraces you, not one that baffles you or bounces you around so that you can't even tell where I'm. And so I have chosen to work, very, very

141

carefully, with the language we share, faults and all, choosing each word for its capacity, its ambiguity, the space it provides for me to live my life within it, relating rather than opposing each word to the next, each sentence to the next, "starting on all sides at once...twenty times, thirty times, over": the stuttering adventure of the essay.

Mairs' aim is to "nullify the splitting—of body from spirit, of critic from creator, of intellect from desire, of self from other..." Of course, it is an admirable goal and one that I should like to aspire to as well. But how to accomplish it. She writes that "I just keep inscribing the fathers' words with my woman's fingers and hope that the feminine will bleed through."

Nancy Mairs has suffered depression, hospitalization, physical disability. About the place that writing holds in her life, she writes:

> I don't mean I took up writing as therapy. Although I don't doubt that writing can have remedial value, I've never been much interested in this aspect of it, maybe because I associate it with my months in a mental hospital, when an occupational therapist labored doggedly to get me to sit in a stuffy little room with some other patients and weave potholders. I didn't want to mend my life. I didn't want to restore my life to its old order. I'd gone through my chaos and dissolution. As I began to grow increasingly calm and watchful, I aimed to experience, with Virginia Woolf, "the strangest feeling now of our all being in the midst of some vast operation; of the splendour of this undertaking--life; of being capable of dying: an immensity surrounds me." I was ready to write another life: out here, on the edge, in the wild. I have. I go on.

The letters I've sent you as part of a therapeutic process have a certain validity, but as a discourse, the letters have freed me from the improvident space of academic thinking that I was so caught up in during the time I was writing my thesis. In the letters, I'm myself. As Nancy Mairs claims, "Feminine discourse is not the language of opposites but a babble of eroticism, attachment, and empathy."

It was interesting that of all the things you might have inquired about after my absence of two weeks, you asked if Sam was upstate. Yes. The house is filled with only women these days. There's a certain peace to be obtained simply by putting some distance between us. Gone is the agonistic struggle to dominate and control, of which I'm a part, I must ruefully admit, since I still try to provide reasons, causality, beginnings, middles, ends to our conversations. Gone the fear and hostility, the cynicism. It's not as if there are no boundaries. We are two women, living together--alone. I find myself returning to some of the most basic pleasures--the garden, my books, music. The pleasure of solving small problems, of breathless anticipation, of carrying out distinctly personal tasks, of calmly making plans. And all within the lassitude of summer's hazy slow rhythms. I'm enjoying the respite. Thank you for the breathing lessons, mon cher.

Tuesday, July 12, 1994

We spoke at our last session about restoring some of the ground rules we'd set prior to my most recent crisis. To be precise, I want to restore your fee to what it was before my daughter entered therapy. I want to do this for several reasons. Just as it's morally right and spiritually empowering to help a friend who, through no fault of her own, is suddenly in desperate circumstances, it's also right for that person to accept help no longer than necessary from her benefactor. You understood my circumstances and responded by adjusting your fee in my favor. If, however, my circumstances change for the better at some future date, am I not obligated to make an adjustment in your favor? In friendship, integrity flows both ways, I would think. Then too, I suppose that I want to do this because I really wish that restitution had been made by those for whom I've made some generous adaptive gesture. There's an old saying in

143

Yiddish -- "don't tell me when you cry, because you don't tell me when you dance." If I tell you when I do both, then I can presume to be an "entitled" friend.

I received word yesterday from my sister-in-law that my uncle died and that the funeral would be held today in Chicago. The news set off any number of recollections, but my immediate reaction was a calm deliberation. I was prepared for this news by the inevitable logic of generations. He was a man of about 80 years of age, with a failing heart. Even had I been notified through legitimate channels of his death (as opposed to my mother's melodramatic message on my answering machine), I would not have returned to Chicago to attend his funeral so soon after having been there for a wedding. No, a note expressing my condolences to my aunt will be sent in a few days and, most importantly, I'll try to write something of what I knew and felt about him and the rest of my mother's family at some safe time in the future. In this way, I'll be able to make sense of, to order this loss among the others, to offer up whatever solace can be taken from language in its imperious command of events. It's the only way I know, the only emolument to apply to a bruised heart.

I've enclosed an article on being a woman and being 50, as well as a page from Nancy Mairs' book. My "I" cannot stop writing for your "you" this week, 'bon ami.
Jusqu'a Samedi

Moi-meme, sain et sauf

Jess

Monday, July 18, 1994

Cher ebon ami,

Why must you continue to view my life on the margin as the "unlived life?" To be sure, it's not the life you'd construct for me, but that makes it no less valid, no less real, no less interesting. Your observation at our last session that I might be horrified by a late "awakening," by the realization of all I've missed of lived life is corrosive to my soul. It eats away at my very core, like acid rain on granite. For if I know anything, I know that I've been a constant witness, an avid observer and so, I have not missed very much of "the life," cher ami.

I'm a late bloomer, it's true, but *I do bloom* -- albeit in shadowy corners of private rooms. I told you I believe in an evolving consciousness. Why can't you see that there's more to "the life" than can be experienced in its immediacy—there's memory and reflection (without which we would have no regret or remorse, two of the moral properties of life), hope and anticipation, solitude and society, dreams and awakenings, revelations and epiphanies, poetry, music, beauty, silence, history, love, hate. And for a view of it all, I choose my vantage point for its refraction of the light, the outer circle. From my vantage point on the margin, I bear witness, I describe, I articulate, I make order out of perceived chaos, I master the hard truths, I adjust, adapt, fashion, imagine, invent, trace and translate -- in short, my dear listener and gentle interrogator, the "you" of "I"—I write. You always forget this about me. Nothing can give more structure to my days than to take up my pen.

I had an eventful weekend -- it was good that I took Friday as a vacation day, a quiet time for catching up with things I'd been putting off. Like correspondence other than these damned letters (they possess me, these letters!). After leaving you on Saturday, I entertained a houseful of people all day and well into the evening. Saturday evening we watched the fireworks display going on in a nearby park from the deck behind the house. The deck that we had built over the concrete foundation for what was to be living quarters for my mother -- how my heart ached whenever I looked out at that bleak deserted site. But now, I take my coffee on the deck, sit in the shade of an umbrella and read the Sunday Times, speak to friends on the phone, cultivate pots and pots of flowers and plants. There are compensations.

Saturday afternoon, Mimi brought home a new kitten to the delight of my company and I must admit myself. We all made much ado of him – love at first sight. He's going to grow up to be quite a handsome cat. His markings are very beautiful – he's all black with the exception of white mittens and boots, a white diamond at his throat and a stripe of white right down his belly!

When everyone left late Saturday evening, I watched the three tenors on television. I must admit I found it to be too commercial a concert for my tastes, but all three gentlemen are so charismatic, I couldn't forego their performance. Then on Sunday morning, I went with a friend to a local pool for a swim. It's one of my favorite pastimes. Unfortunately, Sunday afternoon, Mimi became ill at the wheel of her car and sideswiped a parked car around the corner from our house. She'd been sunbathing at the zenith of the day, drank a cold drink and took her medication before going for a drive with a friend. I question whether she's aware of the strength of the medication she's taking, as well as the wisdom of some of her actions. Nevertheless, she very responsibly went over and spoke with the owner of the car she had swiped and today, she called her father herself and told him about the accident. I've always known that Mimi and Sam communicate better with each other than either does with me. I was relieved to be left out of this one, fraught as I am with fears about both of them acting out of control.

On Sunday evening, I went over to Lenny's house and worked on a resume for a woman ad executive, the mother of a friend of mine. It was interesting to see how other women deal with the issue of age in the workplace. I feel as if I've helped her by working up her resume and cover letter so that age as knowledge and experience becomes a positive factor in her job search rather than a setback. She said I'd taken a burden off her after our initial interview. Many of my clients tell me that they feel relieved after they've met with me and worked up their resume.

So you see, it was a busy weekend for me, but not without its high points. Oh, yes, I received a letter from my mother, enclosing my uncle's obituary and giving me the gory details of his demise and outlining her martyrdom during his last days. For

God sakes, the man was 80 years old -- he had to die of something! She is morbid, as only self-absorbed people can be morbid. She spares no opportunity for shaking the bones over my head!

When I was six years old, my mother left my father and we went to live with my grandfather. This had the most profound influence on my young life. But that is another story for another evening, 'bon ami. I'm afraid the heat in my study overcomes my passion to disabuse myself of family secrets!

I think of you often. I know you are there.

Jusqu'a Samedi,

Moi-meme, sain et sauf

Jess

At the next session, he brought up the letters again. He said that he'd gone through my file and that he felt he should never have encouraged my writing the letters. After rereading them, however, he could not bring himself to destroy them. I felt convinced that he'd been reviewed and that someone, perhaps a mentor or a supervisor had advised him about the liability the letters might become as part of a patient's file. At the same time, he was very gently disengaging from our weekly meetings. I was unprepared to give up the letters, much more the relationship that had acted as a lifeline during my daughter's illness and the shallows of my marriage. Nevertheless, it would be so. And I had something now that I'd never had before. I had the letters—they were mine.

Saturday, July 23, 1994

Cher ebon ami,

It seems to me by our recent talks that you're burdened by the intimacy of the letters and by the notion of confidentiality and your professional obligation to me as a patient, as well as to your profession in general and to yourself.

Well, I suppose I've also been looking for a way to bring our correspondence to closure. It has, after all, always exceeded our face to face relationship in its intimacy and I think that maybe in that respect it can only complicate a straightforward doctor patient relationship. And I think we would both agree that whatever serves to obscure or detract from a positive therapy shouldn't continue. Besides, I feel that without the letters, we'll be more apt to make our actual sessions more fruitful. Writing, after all, is a construction, an imaginative space, that, because of its temporality, provides me limitless possibilities to defend and protect myself, as open and spontaneous conversation cannot do.

Your suggestion, however, that I begin to keep a journal which I can transform into a book at some future date about this interactive therapy seems to me to be wishful thinking. It's a little like advising me to undergo *in vitro* fertilization when I sit before you great with child. The book *exists*, it's written and continues to be written in the form of a collection of letters. Since there's no written response to the letters from you, they're more a soliloquy than anything else. But they are in no way gratuitous. During the time in which they were composed and within the context of this therapy, I've become a writer and freed myself of the restrictions and limitations both self-imposed and imposed by external events that prevented me from this sort of expression. My writing from this point forward will undoubtedly be different because I've written these letters. In short, there's a considerable investment of self in them for me and they've rendered me a considerable reward.

Of course, you've been most sensitive, discreet and shown the utmost courtesy and sophistication as their recipient. It's simply that the public and the private domains are not so precisely drawn for me as they must be for you, and in the case of the letters, at some point they took flight, became a figment of my imagination, having almost nothing to do with the reality of our face to face relationship (for instance, I call again and again upon a male archetype in the letters with whom I'm far more intimate than I am with you).

148

And in fact, for a while now, there's been a third party to the letters. Much of their composition plays to an anonymous audience (probably made up of other women). No, 'bon ami, we're no longer alone in the letters. There are others whom I hope are listening—listening and understanding. It's as if I'm speaking to you on the phone with an entire shadowy host sitting before me. My words are for you, but they're also for them. Perhaps this is simply a growing awareness, an enhanced consciousness of myself, but I would wish with all my heart that it's more than that.

As to the disposition of the letters in your files, you may, of course, destroy them and retain only your notes on our visits. I would think that this would be a true record of my progress as your patient and all that is necessary for any official or unofficial scrutiny of your files. Our "real" friendship will be in no way diminished by this or any other superficial act of housecleaning or record keeping. You know that I trust you implicitly—how else would I have put my fine insanity into your keeping these several times—and I'm flattered and touched by your remark that you can't bring yourself at this point to dispose of my letters. It says quite a lot about who we both are and who we've become in each other's company that you would feel that way.

As to your suggestion for an alternative to the letters, I've never been a diarist or a journal keeper. It's too inner directed an activity for me, too stultifying, in my opinion. Like talking to myself. And I don't recall as a child ever having had a secret or imaginary friend, from which to spin off a "pen pal" or correspondent.

No, there's no precedent for the letters and it's unlikely that there will be any subsequent correspondence. Writing to you takes up a great deal of whatever time I have for writing anything at all. There are the days after our session when I think about what I will write, then two or three days of actual composition, and there you are, I'm back in your office again! Yes, they do help to fill in between visits, but the letters have grown much weightier and infinitely more important than this simple rationale for their existence. They speak to what is basically good and noble in each of us and also of an abiding wish to communicate, to make our utterances count as art and therapy. They do connect us to each other in a very unique way, (having originated as they did out of a simple misunderstanding between us) traversing our differences. I'll miss writing them to you, 'bon ami, as I'm sure you'll miss receiving them. I am grateful to have had your ear for even this amount of time.

Jusqu'a Samedi,

Moi-meme, sain et sauf

Jess

Epilogue

Saturday, December 3, 1994

Mon vieux,

Finally I'm able to write to you. My everyday life is so filled with burdensome situations, responsibilities and worry these days, I literally must carve out a time for writing. It was so pleasant to speak with you the other day. Of course, we had to get beyond the tensions and stress we both live under, but then we were fine. I was left with the feeling that what we both needed more than anything else was the soothing balm of human connection, l'amitie.

I think what's missing in the press of your work is that quality you possess of elegant courtesy. We aren't very courteous here in the States; we feel we have no time for the courtesies of everyday life. But you, despite your successful adaptation to our culture, remain very Haitian at the core. Right now, you lack the providential space to pursue the form and structure of courtesy that's so much a part of your nature and that seems to make possible the epiphanies by which you grow and learn. I'm reading a wonderful book by Mary Catherine Bateson, who is the daughter of famed anthropologist, Margaret Mead. It's called *Peripheral Visions*. Bateson says, "Courtesy is one of the great human inventions for bridging uncertainty."

Ah, well, my good doctor, it is tres drole, don't you think, for me to be analyzing you. Far better I think to bring you up to date on my life and share with you those fortuitous vacation days I recently spent in the Caribbean. It was my sixth or seventh visit to this island that lies just where two tradewinds meet. A lucky place, I told myself, aware that elsewhere in the Caribbean Sea, Hurricane Gordon was wreaking havoc, while in places like Puerta Vallarta, tourists were sweltering in unrelenting heat.

Day one was spent in a sort of torpor on a beach chair before a very blue expanse of water. Each time I opened my eyes, the scene reconfirmed in my memory this favorite place, this island.

151

An immense feeling of renewal, of the re-emergence of a latent, but authentic self overwhelmed me. Our expectations for this vacation had been thwarted almost immediately at the airport when we were refused an upgrade to first class given to GM by her employer—a gesture of his gratitude. At the last minute we were granted the upgrade, but of course, it required a great deal of running back and forth from gate to information desk in the terminal. Finally we boarded and enjoyed all the amenities promised, but not without first being made to feel that we were usurpers of privilege, interlopers in an inner sanctum reserved for a special and worthy few.

But the hotel we're staying at this year is lovely. When we walked into the open air lobby Thursday evening and I saw once again, the muted colors, the palms moving in a gentle breeze, the rich carpets on smooth earthen tile floors, when I smelled the scent of perfume in the air, I was so thankful to have come again to this island. For the aesthetics of place have been important to me for as long as I can remember. And those places that speak to the rich visions that delight the inner eye, remain forever in my heart. This island is one of them. Italy another.

But I go on and on about my vacation. I hope that you and your family have a wonderful holiday like this one was and soon, mon medecin bon, soon. You should learn to make your own providential space. I think of you whenever or wherever I find mine.

Adieu
Tess
L'ancienne

About The Author

Suzanne Rubinstein has been making things up since she was a girl in Chicago. Only recently, however, has she begun to write them down. Having lived and worked in New York long enough to appreciate it as the greathearted city it is, she makes her debut here with a collection of letters that cross the boundaries of race, gender and culture.

Ms Rubinstein holds a Masters degree in Womens Studies from The Graduate School of the City University of New York. She is currently working on a series of short stories set in a Catskill mountain resort that has seen better days. She lives with one musician and one cat. She has three daughters.